D1432785

STUDIES IN GERMAN LITERATURE,
LINGUISTICS, AND CULTURE
Vol. 45

Music, Love, Death and Mann's *Dr. Faustus*

JOHN FRANCIS FETZER

Music, Love, Death

and Mann's *Doctor Faustus*

CAMDEN HOUSE

Set in Times Roman and printed on acid-free paper.

Library of Congress Cataloging-in-Publication Data

Fetzer, John F.
    Music, love, death, and Mann's Doctor Faustus / by John Francis
Fetzer.
        p.   cm. -- (Studies in German literature, linguistics, and
culture ; v. 45)
    Includes bibliographical references.
    ISBN 0-938100-71-8
    1. Music in literature. 2. Love in literature. 3. Death in
literature.   [1. Mann, Thomas, 1875-1955. Doktor Faustus.]
I. Title. II. Series.
PT2625.A44D6935   1989
833'.912--dc20   89-23887
                                                             CIP

To Susan and Darrell
for
patience and forebearance over the years

Contents

Acknowledgments

I owe a great debt of gratitude to the Office of Research of the University of California, Davis, for its generous assistance over the years, even when concrete results were not immediately forthcoming. Indirectly I am also indebted to the John Simon Guggenheim Foundation for a 1981 grant in support of another project — a study entitled *On the Threshold of German Romanticism*. The leave-time which the Guggenheim Fellowship afforded me provided the opportunity to devote my attention again to Thomas Mann's *Doktor Faustus* after a hiatus of too many years.

A word of sincere appreciation is also due my undaunted word-processing whiz, Yvonne S. Unnold, for her time and talents. She mastered the stringent requirements of formatting, indexing, etc. which would have consumed an inordinate amount of time had I, an inveterate computer illiterate, been obliged to fathom the mysteries of this miraculous instrument.

Preface

THE ORIGINS OF THIS monograph lie in the confluence of two seemingly divergent experiences. The first is a long-abiding fascination for the reciprocal links between music, love, and death, a tripartite configuration which can be subsumed under the Greek designations: Melos-Eros-Thanatos. Recourse to Greek etymological roots to describe the kinship between music, love, and death seems justified in view of Homer's saga of the sirens or Orpheus' mythical rescue mission to wrest his beloved Eurydice from the underworld. These figures, together with their modern German counterparts in the Romantics' "Loreley" and Rilke's Thracian poet-singer in the *Sonnets to Orpheus*, have interested me subliminally for about three decades. The second — and most immediate — catalyst for this study was the series of Harvard Lectures which Leonard Bernstein delivered originally in 1974. I heard these talks, published as *The Unanswered Question*, for the first time in 1981 on German television and in German translation. While residing in the idyllic hamlet of Buchenbach on the outskirts of Freiburg im Breisgau, I reread Thomas Mann's novel of 1947, *Doctor Faustus. The Life of the German Composer Adrian Leverkühn as Told by a Friend*.[1] Concurrent with this I listened to Bernstein expound on modern music. Strange bedfellows at first glance, perhaps, Bernstein and Mann; but not really so. For as I watched the articulate American composer-conductor-musicologist develop themes such as "The Delights and Dangers of Ambiguity" or "The Twentieth Century Crisis,"[2] I was vividly reminded of passages by the German novelist which grappled with similar musical phenomena. Suddenly things began to jell in my mind in that exciting fashion which, on rare occasions, dominates one's entire thinking process. Instead of turning to the research project for which I had specifically come to Germany, I re-turned, with Bernstein as my cicerone, to the

---

[1] Trans. from the German *Doktor Faustus. Das Leben des deutschen Tonsetzers Adrian Leverkühn erzählt von einem Freunde* by H.T. Lowe-Porter (New York: The Modern Library, 1948). All subsequent English quotations from the novel are taken from this Modern Library edition and indicated directly in the text, followed by the reference to the corresponding page(s) in volume VI of the edition *Thomas Mann: Gesammelte Werke in zwölf Bänden* (Frankfurt am Main: S. Fischer, 1960 ff), where the parallel German text can be found. For example, a reference to page 47 of the English translation would be: (47/VI 66). References to other volumes in the *Gesammelte Werke in zwölf Bänden* will be treated in a similar manner; for example, volume IX, 202, would be (IX 202). For the convenience of the reader, an appendix containing all the quotations from *Doctor Faustus* in the original German has been included. Unless otherwise indicated, translations from primary and secondary sources other than *Faustus* are my own.

[2] Leonard Bernstein, *The Unanswered Question: Six Talks at Harvard* (Cambridge, Massachusetts: Harvard University Press, 1976).

music, love, and death constellation. The result of this spontaneous synthesis of old interests and new insights, of literary hypothesis and musical analysis, was the present investigation, which proved effective in isolating one of the building blocks of the *Doctor Faustus* novel. The question to be answered then was: Could the cornerstone of Melos-Eros-Thanatos support a structural framework on which to erect a cohesive interpretation of that monumental work?

One pertinent example of the way in which the Harvard lectures and the novel dovetailed in my mind lies in the term "ambiguity," on which Bernstein focuses extensively and which he illustrates musically with reference to Wagner's *Tristan und Isolde*. In Mann's novel, the composer Adrian Leverkühn, early in his career as the bedeviled creator and innovator of modern music, declares to his life-long acquaintance, Serenus Zeitblom, Ph.D., the de facto narrator of the book: "'Relationship is everything. And if you want to give it a more precise name, it is ambiguity.... You know what I find? ... That music turns the equivocal into a system'" (47/VI 66). Equivocation as the *modus operandi* unique to music will also be shown to obtain in the spheres of love and death as they are portrayed in this novel. Consequently, all three components in the title of this monograph share the characteristic of ambiguity as a common denominator.[3]

The "twentieth-century crisis," which Bernstein surveys in his lectures with respect to music, naturally forms an essential ingredient in a work of fiction having as its protagonist a problematic, modern composer. The element of "crisis" in Melos likewise manifests itself with regard to the other two components of the constellation, Eros and Thanatos. It is a fundamental contention of this study that the entire tripartite complex, the interdependence of music, love, and death, enters a critical stage on the threshold of our century. Whereas the constituent elements still function in interaction with each other, a radical juxtaposition or transvaluation has taken place. The result is that any aura of uplifting spiritual transcendence, any sense that, even in view of the demise of one or both of the "star crossed" lovers, the tragic dimension has, in some fashion, been alleviated by the power of music, diminishes. The days of the romantic "death and transfiguration" have passed. The "dismemberment" of the modern Orpheus is not necessarily followed by his ascension to a higher sphere of activity. As an aftermath of such a development, other questions inevitably arise. Once an author such as Mann has delineated the end of a myth, much as Wagner had chronicled the twilight of the gods, is there, in the wake of such a grim diagnosis, any positive prognosis? And with specific

---

[3] See, for instance, the section "The Delights and Dangers of Ambiguity" in Bernstein, *The Unanswered Question*, 227-37.

reference to the triad of Melos-Eros-Thanatos in its twentieth-century phase of deconstruction: does it serve as a kind of barometer for measuring other value systems inherited from the past which fail to stand the test of time, or which falter when, in our own time, they are put to the test?

1   The Music-Love-Death Triad: A Synoptic Glance at the Melos-Eros-Thanatos Configuration from Mythical to Modern Times

EVEN THOUGH COMPARATIVE STUDIES treating Thomas Mann and music are legion, those dealing with this writer's approach to death have appeared only periodically, while analyses of his attitude toward love have, until recent years, been quite sporadic and rare.[1] Occasionally, particularly in the present decade, investigations of the love-death or "Liebestod" linkage in Mann have come to the fore, but even in these instances, the musical component seldom proves to be a major factor.[2] Consequently, it is not surprising that the intimate correlation of all three elements in Mann's oeuvre has gone virtually unheeded by scholars, except for an oblique aside or parenthetical remark. The following study seeks to fill this lacuna, without intruding extensively on the material already in print dealing with Melos, Eros, Thanatos as separate entities in their own right.[3]

---

[1] Although quantity is not necessarily an indicator of quality, the sheer bulk of scholarship devoted to musical matters as opposed to the other two topics gives a clear indication of where the major focal point of interest lies - or has lain. Statistics for the period prior to 1980 garnered from the major bibliographical sources on Mann (Klaus Jonas, *Die Thomas-Mann-Literatur. Band I: Bibliographie der Kritik 1896-1955* [Berlin: Erich Schmidt, 1972]; Band II: *Bibliographie der Kritik 1956-1975* [Berlin: Erich Schmidt, 1979]; Harry Matter, *Die Literatur über Thomas Mann. Eine Bibliographie 1898-1969* [Berlin: Aufbau, 1972]; Hermann Kurzke, *Thomas-Mann-Forschung 1969-1976. Ein kritischer Bericht* [Frankfurt am Main: S. Fischer, 1977], Clemens Köttelwesch, *Bibliographie der deutschen Sprach- und Literaturwissenschaft*, vols. 17-20 for the years 1977-1980 [Frankfurt am Main: Klostermann, 1978-1981] and *Germanistik*, vols. 18-21 for the years 1977-1980]) indicate the following approximate distribution: 298 studies of music, 17 dealing with love and 65 treating death. For the period 1981-1986, vols. 21-26 of the Köttelwesch *Bibliographie* and *Germanistik*, vols. 22-29 (1981-1988) reveal the following statistics: Music: 31 Love: 18 Death: 7.

[2] Note, for example, the generalized overview by James Northcote-Bade, "The Background to the 'Liebestod' Plot Pattern in the Works of Thomas Mann," *Germanic Review* 59 (1984): 11-18; Martin Gregor-Dellin, "Tristan. Faszination für einen Dichter," in Gregor-Dellin, *Richard Wagner. Die Revolution als Oper* (Munich: Hanser, 1973): 88-97, and the perceptive article by Gerhard Schulz, "Liebestod: The Literary Background of Wagner's *Tristan und Isolde*," *Miscellanea Musicologica* (Adelaide Studies in Musicology) 14 (1985): 118-29.

[3] In spite of earlier investigations of the erotic aspect of Mann's oeuvre such as Frank Hirschbach's *The Arrow and the Lyre: A Study of the Role of Love in the Works of Thomas Mann* (The Hague; Nijhoff, 1955) or the chapter on love and homoeroticism in Ignace

Music, Love, Death and Mann's *Doctor Faustus*

The neglect of this triadic nucleus as a tri-unity or total "package," so to speak, is striking, in view of its venerable history in Western literature, extending back to such mythic figures as Orpheus. The tale of this ancient Greek bard, whose enchanting lyre tones enable him to win back his beloved Eurydice from the realm of the Plutonian shades, only to lose her forever on the threshold between upper and lower realms, might serve as the mythical prototype for a host of accounts in which music is closely allied with the erotic and the thanatotic.[4] From medieval to modern times there were epochs in which this triple alliance flourished: the courtly Minnesingers come to mind, as do the poets of the baroque and the romantic ages. One might also cite such a familiar passage as that which opens Shakespeare's *Twelfth Night*: "If music be the food of love, play on,/ Give me excess of it; that, surfeiting,/ The appetite may sicken, and so die."[5] To be sure, the linking of love, music, and death in these verses functions as a virtual conceit, a literary topos. But as such, it registers the extent to which the triadic constellation had become a

---

Feuerlicht's *Thomas Mann und die Grenzen des Ich* (Heidelberg: Winter, 1966), Herbert Lehnert, in his comprehensive analysis of the major critical literature, *Thomas-Mann-Forschung: Ein Bericht* (Stuttgart: Metzler, 1969), 115, expressed dissatisfaction with the treatment of "the extraordinarily strong love motif in Thomas Mann's work." This situation has been remedied considerably in the interim since Lehnert's report by the appearance of such investigations as: Inta Miske Ezergailis, *Male and Female: An Approach to Thomas Mann's Dialectic* (The Hague: Nijhoff, 1975), Eckhard Heftrich, *Vom Verfall zur Apokalypse. Über Thomas Mann.* Band II (Frankfurt am Main: Klostermann, 1982), especially the chapter "Eros und Politik," 114-28; Claus Sommerhage, *Eros und Poesis. Über das Erotische im Werk Thomas Manns* (Bonn: Bouvier, 1983), Mechthild Curtius, *Erotische Phantasien bei Thomas Mann* (Königstein: Athenäum, 1984), Frederick Albrecht Lubich, *Die Dialektik von Logos und Eros im Werk von Thomas Mann* (Heidelberg: Winter, 1986), and Gerhard Härle, *Die Gestalt des Schönen. Untersuchungen zur Homosexualitätsthematik in Thomas Manns Roman 'Der Zauberberg'*. Hochschulschriften: Literaturwissenschaft, Bd. 74 (Königstein: Hain, 1986). With specific reference to Doctor Faustus, one should note: Steven Cerf, "Love in Thomas Mann's Doctor Faustus as an Imitatio Shakespeari," *Comparative Literature Studies* 18 (1981): 475-86, as well as specific sections of the aforementioned works (as, for instance, 115-58 in Hirschbach and 238-77 in Sommerhage).

[4] For a treatment of the Orpheus myth and its specific relation to modern literature, see Ihab Hassan, *The Dismemberment of Orpheus: Toward a Postmodern Literature* (New York: Oxford University Press, 1971).

[5] *Twelfth Night or What You Will*, Act I, Scene 1, lines 1-3 in the edition *The Works of Shakespeare*, ed. Sir Arthur Quiller-Couch and John Dover Wilson (Cambridge, England: Cambridge University Press, 1968), 3. For an analysis of the function of this play in relation to *Doctor Faustus*, see Steven Cerf, "The Shakespearean Element in Thomas Mann's *Doktor Faustus*-Montage," *Revue de Littérature Comparée* 59 (1985): 427-41.

commonplace readily grasped by Shakespearean audiences. This formulation, today a *locus classicus* in literature, plays a sub rosa role in the interpretation of Mann's *Doctor Faustus*. In this novel, certain aspects of Shakespeare's dramaturgy coalesce with the forces of music, love and death, to articulate for the twentieth century reader a drastic, almost apocalyptic variant of the Melos-Eros-Thanatos constellation.

Before focusing attention on Mann's *Doctor Faustus* of 1947, however, it might be informative to take a preliminary glance at his earlier fiction, specifically the novella *Tristan* (1903). The comparison reveals an interplay between traditional attitudes toward the correlation of music, love, and death, as well as the incipient, but unmistakable signs of disenfranchisement to which these concepts would eventually be subjected. The titles of the respective works — *Doctor Faustus* and *Tristan* — are in themselves significant insofar as each can claim a dual ancestry in the history of German literature and culture. In the case of the latter work, Gottfried von Straßburg's unfinished courtly epic of ca. 1210, *Tristan und Isôt*, and Richard Wagner's music drama of 1859, *Tristan und Isolde*, were the most dominant predecessors.[6] For the former, on the other

[6] The Wagnerian ties to Mann's novella have been examined quite extensively: Martin Gregor-Dellin, *Wagner und kein Ende. Richard Wagner im Spiegel von Thomas Manns Prosawerk* (Bayreuth: Edition Musica, 1958), 184-94, "Wagners *Tristan* bei Thomas Mann"; Erwin Koppen, *Dekadenter Wagnerismus. Studien zur europäischen Literatur des Fin de siècle,* Komparatistische Studien, Beihefte zu *Arcadia*, vol. 2 (Berlin: de Gruyter, 1973); James Northcote-Bade, *Die Wagner-Mythen im Frühwerk Thomas Manns* (Bonn: Bouvier, 1975), Chapter III: *"Tristan und Isolde* und *Tristan,"* 39-52; Stevie Anne Bolduc, "A Study of Intertextuality: Thomas Mann's *Tristan* and Richard Wagner's *Tristan und Isolde," Rocky Mountain Review* 37 (1983): 82-90; Horst Albert Glaser, "Wagners Musik im Werk Thomas Manns," in *Richard Wagner 1883-1983*, ed. Ursula Müller, Stuttgarter Arbeiten zur Germanistik, Bd. 129 (Stuttgart: Heinz, 1984), 411-31; Eckhard Heftrich, "Richard Wagner im Werk Thomas Manns," *Hefte der Deutschen Thomas-Mann-Gesellschaft, Sitz Lübeck* 5 (1985): 5-18. With specific reference to *Faustus*, see George W. Reinhardt, "Thomas Mann's *Doctor Faustus*: A Wagnerian Novel," *Mosaic* 18 (1985): 109-23 and Mary A. Cicora, "Wagner Parody in *Doctor Faustus," The Germanic Review* 63 (1988): 133-39. On the other hand, the possible links - direct or indirect - to Gottfried von Straßburg's original courtly epic have not aroused much scholarly attention. Michael Batts, for instance, in his panoramic survey "Tristan and Isolde in Modern Literature: L'éternel retour," *Seminar* 5 (1969): 79-90, does not even mention Mann's novella. In his study *Der Zauberer. Das Leben des deutschen Schriftstellers Thomas Mann*, vol. I (Frankfurt am Main: S. Fischer, 1975), 175-77, Peter de Mendelssohn gives an account of Mann's attendance at Wilhelm von Hertz's lectures on the German medieval epic (including *Tristan*) in Munich (1894), and Mann himself remarked in an explanatory note to a plot summary of *Tristan*, which he wrote for a projected film version of 1923, that this adaptation was not based on Wagner's opera, but rather on Gottfried's

hand, the Dr. Faustus chapbook of 1587 and Goethe's lifelong *Faust* tragedy served as milestones to be consulted and confronted.[7] Whereas for the *Tristan* tale, a greater influence on Mann was exerted by the nineteenth-century music-drama than by the medieval romance, in the case of *Faustus*, the chronological inverse holds true. The sixteenth-century chapbook far outstrips Goethe's *Faust* (1832) in Mann's modern adaptation of the legend. Yet the six decades in which Goethe's monumental work was conceived and completed, 1770-1831, represent the years of Storm and Stress and the Classic-Romantic period. These intellectual trends imbued the novel with such dominant musical overtones and literary undertones, that this factor must be borne in mind when tracing precedents and antecedents.[8]

"ingenious poem, to which I had never before been so close" (XIII 18). For the latest analysis of this project, see Herbert Kolb, "Über Thomas Manns Filmexposé 'Tristan und Isolde,' " in *Romantik und Moderne, Neue Beiträge aus Forschung und Lehre. Festschrift für Helmut Motekat*, ed. Erich Hubert-Thomas and Ghemela Adler (Frankfurt am Main: Lang, 1986), 303-27. Peter Wapnewski in the chapter "Tristan, keine Burleske. Zu Thomas Manns Novelle" from his book *Tristan der Held Richard Wagners* (Berlin: Severin and Seidler, 1981) observes that in Gottfried's epic the social component (the deception of Marke as King) dominates over the moral issue (Marke as the husband), while in Mann's work neither of the conflicts is solved or resolved, but rather given definitive form of expression for our age (the problem of infidelity, for example, was a standard element in European décadence and has become an integral aspect of our social structure).

[7] In this connection, see Birgit S. Nielsen, "Adrian Leverkühns Leben als bewußte mythische imitatio des Doktor Faustus," *Orbis Litterarum* 20 (1965): 128-58; Dietrich Assmann, *Thomas Manns Roman 'Doktor Faustus' und seine Beziehungen zur Faust Tradition* (Helsinki: Suomalainen Tiedeakatemia, 1975); Lieselotte Voss, *Die Entstehung von Thomas Manns Roman 'Doktor Faustus'*, Studien zur deutschen Literatur, 39 (Tübingen: Niemeyer, 1975) and, most recently, Marguerite De Huszar Allen, *The Faust Legend: Popular Form and the Modern Novel*, Germanic Studies in America, vol. 53 (New York: Lang, 1985). Even Mann's agreement with a critic in 1948 that he had produced "the most un-Goethean of all Fausts" is tinged with a sense of coming to terms with Goethe, only if indirectly by negation (*Dichter über ihre Dichtungen: Thomas Mann*, Vol. 14/Part III, ed. Hans Wysling in collaboration with Marianne Fischer [Munich: Heimeran, 1981], 135). See also in this connection, Joachim Müller, "Faustus und Faust. Thomas Manns Roman und Goethes Tragödie," *Universitas* 16 (1961): 731-43.

[8] For some general references, see Hans Eichner, "Thomas Mann und die deutsche Romantik," in *Das Nachleben der Romantik in der modernen deutschen Literatur*, ed. Wolfgang Paulsen (Heidelberg: Stiehm, 1969), 152-73; Helmut Brandt, "Thomas Mann und die deutsche Romantik," in *Werk und Wirkung Thomas Manns in unserer Epoche. Ein internationaler Dialog*, ed. Helmut Brandt and Hans Kaufmann (Berlin: Aufbau, 1978), 117-39 and, with specific reference to *Doktor Faustus*, Gerhard vom Hofe, "Das unbehagliche Bewußtsein des

The Tradition of the Music-Love-Death Triad

Without probing extensively into the details of either Gottfried's epic techniques or Wagner's musico-literary devices in their respective *Tristan* adaptions, one should at least take a cursory look at the reciprocity of Melos-Eros-Thanatos in each. Such an overview, augmented by a glance at several other seminal works in German literature, will establish certain general guidelines and lay the groundwork for Mann's modifications of what he inherited. Having done this, one can then pinpoint what he either endorsed in his own *Tristan* or viewed through the prismatic lens of an ironically altered perspective.

In Gottfried's iconoclastically unchivalric courtly *Tristan* romance, the erotic component becomes all-pervasive.[9] The thanatotic concept is latent in the marriage à trois situation, and voiced in allusions to an "illicit" love bond such as that of Tristan and Isolde being tantamount to societal or ethical "death."[10] The musical constituent expresses itself in the melodic ebb and

---

modernen Musikers. Zu Wackenroders Berglinger und Thomas Manns *Doktor Faustus*," in *Geist und Zeichen. Festschrift für Arthur Henkel*, ed. Herbert Anton, Bernhard Gajek and Peter Pfaff (Heidelberg: Winter, 1977), 144-56.

[9] For an analysis of the erotic dimension of the work, see W.T.H. Jackson, *The Anatomy of Love: The "Tristan" of Gottfried von Straßburg* (New York: Columbia University Press, 1971), especially Chapter IV: "Aspects of Love," 64-161. With regard to the musical components of this love relationship, see specifically 76 and 128. The most recent research on the subject is: Hugo Bekker, *Gottfried's Tristan: Journey through the Realm of Eros*. Studies in German Literature, Language, and Culture, vol. 29 (Columbia, SC: Camden House, 1987). The nature of the erotic in literature on a more broad-based scope can be traced in the standard work by Denis de Rougement, *L'Amour et l'occident*, 2nd ed. (Paris: Plon, 1956) as well as in more recent studies such as *Liebe als Literatur. Aufsätze zur erotischen Dichtung in Deutschland*, ed. Rüdiger Krohn (Munich: Beck, 1983), and Northrop Frye, "The Survival of Eros in Poetry," in *Romanticism and Contemporary Criticism*, ed. Morris Eaves and Michael Fischer (Ithaca, N.Y.: Cornell University Press, 1986), 15-45. With regard to the interrelationship of the Melos-Eros components, see Marcel Brion, *La Musique et l'amour* (Paris: Hachette, 1967) and the chapter "The Musical Erotic" in Alex Aronson, *Music and the Novel: A Study in Twentieth-Century Fiction* (Totowa, New Jersey: Rowman and Littlefield, 1980), 110-36.

[10] In Gottfried's epic, Tristan plays on the interchangeability of love and death when informed by Isolde's handmaid, Brangäne, that the love potion she bears could be fatal:

> "Come what may," said Tristan, ". . . this death suits me well! If my adorable Isolde were to go on being the death of me in this fashion I would woo death everlasting!"

(*Gottfried von Straßburg. Tristan*, trans. with an intro. by A.T. Hatto [Baltimore: Penguin, 1960], 206). Herman Kurzke, in *Thomas Mann. Epoche - Werk - Wirkung* (Munich: Beck,

9

flow of the language rather than in specific imagery or ideational content.[11] Nevertheless, Gottfried does stress Tristan's mastery of musical instruments. One critic notes that in the scene in the love grotto, the protagonist and his lady "engage in a form of music which gives a metaphysical dimension to their amorous play."[12] Undoubtedly the writer has in mind a passage such as the following, in which Gottfried describes how the lovers

> slipped into their refuge and resumed their well-tried pleasure of sounding their harp, and singing sadly and sweetly. They busied their hands and their tongues in turn. They performed amorous lays and their accompaniments, varying their delight as it suited them: for if one took the harp it was for the other to sing the tune with wistful tenderness. And indeed the strains of both harp and tongue, merging their sound in each other, echoed in that cave so sweetly that it was dedicated to sweet Love...[13]

The entire music, love, and death configuration in Gottfried's epic is cast into a somewhat ambiguous light, however, when Tristan later deserts this Isôt (of Kurnewal) and directs his attention as well as his singing to another woman of the same name, Isôt von Arundêl. The exact identity of the addressee to whom his ardent songs are henceforth directed hovers in a limbo of ambivalence. This compromises for the reader the integrity of Tristan's fervent musical declaration of love unto death:

> Tristan composed for every sort of strings many lays and much fine music that have been well loved ever since. It was at this time that he made the noble lay of 'Tristan', which will be treasured and esteemed in every land so long as the world

---

1985), 109 notes in conjunction with Wagner's *Tristan*: "Unconditional love is, just as death, a metaphysical force which is not compatible with earthly existence." Gerhard Schulz in "Liebestod," 128, comments that it is "love which becomes the medium for transcendence.... love, if regarded in such ultimate terms as an absolute quality surpassing all limitations of human existence, must fail within mundane reality. Death is the inevitable companion of absolute love when it attempts to replace the absolutes of religious faith."

[11] Louise Gnaedinger in *Musik und Minne im 'Tristan' Gottfrieds von Straßburg*, Beihefte zur Zeitschrift *Wirkendes Wort*, 1 (Düsseldorf: Schwann, 1967), 7 argues that music in this work is no mere accoutrement or "insinuating, infatuating siren's song," but rather an element intimately and inextricably linked to the essence of the epic and to its protagonists.

[12] Gnaedinger, *Musik und Minne*, 85.

[13] Hatto, *Tristan*, 267.

remains.... When the Court was sitting all together ... he would compose love-songs, rondels and courtly little airs, and always bring in this refrain:

> 'Isôt ma drue, Isôt m'amie,
> en vûs ma mort, en vûs ma vie'!

And since he so loved to sing it, they were all taken up with the idea that he had their Isolde in mind....[14]

The French couplet from Tristan's song ("Isolde my mistress, Isolde my beloved, in you my life, in you my death") runs through the later pages of the unfinished epic almost like a leitmotif. Even though Gottfried seems to disapprove of the behavior of his hero as the epitome of deception, critics have tempered his view. Due to the insoluble nature of the dilemma facing Tristan (the impossibility of living with or without the original Isolde), music, because of the inherent ambiguity of its message, becomes the ideal medium through which to articulate this paradoxical condition.

Between Gottfried's unfinished epic (ca. 1210) and Wagner's music drama (1859) lie not only more than six hundred years of complex intellectual history, but also shifting aesthetic and artistic trends. These treat the interrelationship of music, love, and death in diverse fashion. For instance, there were epochs of emotional restraint and rational domination, such as the Enlightenment, when the tripartite constellation moved from the forefront to the periphery of interest (even though it never disappeared completely from the literary repertoire). On the other hand, the apotheosis of the secularized trinity occurred in the romantic era in Germany, with its early manifestations in Friedrich Schlegel and Novalis or its later modifications in E.T.A. Hoffmann. The culminating point was Wagner's triumphant musicalization of the *Tristan* legend as a kind of tour de force "total work of art."

The dimensions and dynamics of change from the medieval to the modern epoch with reference to the correlation of music, love, and death can be measured by the yardstick of Romanticism. In Schlegel's much heralded novel *Lucinde* (1799), which seeks to put the union of male and female on an emotional rather than an institutional basis, we hear of the "artless, pure, deep accents in music, which the ear does not hear, but rather seems to drink in when the soul thirsts for love."[15] At the core of this innovative work, in the

---

[14] Hatto, *Tristan*, 293.

[15] *Kritische Friedrich-Schlegel-Ausgabe*, ed. Ernst Behler together with Jean-Jacques Anstett

section dealing with the apprenticeship to manhood of the hero, Julius, the latter vows to drown himself in music, "which for him was a dangerous, bottomless abyss of longing and melancholy, into which he willingly would submerge himself."[16] But whereas one hears much about the affinities of music, love, and death in this work, the bond between them still seems more rhetorical than real.

It is rather in Novalis' *Hymnen an die Nacht* (*Hymns to the Night*) (1800) and *Heinrich von Ofterdingen* (1801), which prefigure poetically the ecstatic musical love-death experienced by Wagner's *Tristan und Isolde* over half a century later, that Romanticism finds the *ne plus ultra* of melodic-erotic-thanatotic correlation.[17] In Heinrich's dream-vision after his first encounter with Mathilde, he observes her sitting in a boat singing a simple song. Suddenly the bark becomes caught up in a whirlpool and Mathilde is drawn beneath the waves (almost an inversion of the mythical song of the Sirens and its devastating effect on passing seamen such as Odysseus). Heinrich plunges into the water to rescue her. When both reach what appears to be solid ground, he again hears her singing the "simple song" and Mathilde, after informing him that they are now safe under the blue waters, seals their eternal union with a kiss and a mysterious word. This romanticized love-death dream has overtones of Orpheus' unprecedented rescue of Eurydice from imminent death via his enchanting melodies. Although transformed into an unpretentious song performed by the female partner, this constitutes a powerful poetic statement of the role of music within the parameters of the love-death framework.

Whereas much of the poignancy of the situation of Heinrich and Mathilde is filtered through the medium of the dream, this familiar romantic device is of less consequence in the realistic milieu of Gottfried Keller's novella *Romeo und Julia auf dem Dorfe* (*A Village Romeo and Juliet*) (1865). The star-crossed lovers, Sali and Vrenchen, recalling the dance music which they had heard the previous happy afternoon at a local festival, seek to set aright a world "out of joint" through their suicidal love-death:

> The silence of their world sang to them and made music in their souls; one could hear the river now down below, murmuring gently and tenderly in its flowing undulation.... They listened a

and Hans Eichner, vol. V: *Lucinde*, ed. Hans Eichner (Paderborn: Schöningh, 1962), 18-19.

[16] *Kritische Friedrich-Schlegel-Ausgabe*, V, 21.

[17] For an account of Mann's acquaintance with the life and works of Friedrich von Hardenberg (Novalis), see Hinrich Siefken, "Thomas Mann. Novalis und die Folgen," in *Deutsche Romantik und das 20. Jahrhundert*, ed. Hanne Castein and Alexander Stillmark (Stuttgart: Heinz, 1986), 121-40.

while to these tones, imagined or real, which originated in the great silence or which they confused with the magical effect of the moonlight....[18]

The love-unto-death bond of Heinrich and Mathilde as well as that of the rustic "Romeo and Juliet," whether arising from the reality of a dream or from a dreamlike reality, have something uplifting about them, a certain edifying quality in spite of the adverse circumstances which portend or actually lead to a tragic outcome.

The pivotal work, however, in which the marriage of music, love, and death reached dazzling heights of physical as well as metaphysical intensity never achieved before or since, is Wagner's *Tristan und Isolde* (1859). The musical component, rather than being manifest thematically or metaphorically as had been the case with Gottfried, can now "speak for itself," as it were. In intimate and inimitable fashion, the orchestral and vocal line accompany the fortunes and misfortunes of the ill-fated pair. In the first act Tristan and Isolde confess their love for each other under the erroneous impression that they have drunk a poisoned draught.[19] The second act articulates Tristan's longing for a permanent union with his beloved in death. The closing act brings the fatal wound inflicted by Melot and Tristan's death in Isolde's arms, followed by her own love-death. The apex of the music drama proves to be Isolde's self-induced, psychogenic "Liebestod."[20] From the standpoint of compositional strategy, this scene concludes with the ultimate resolution to diatonic tonality of the musical score after hours of restless surging, constantly shifting chromatic chords and enharmonic orchestral-vocal progressions.

[18] *Gottfried Kellers Werke*, ed. Harry Maync, vol. IV (Berlin: Propyläen, n.d.), 138.

[19] Gunilla Bergsten in *Thomas Mann's Doctor Faustus: The Sources and Structure of the Novel*, trans. Krishna Winston (Chicago: The University of Chicago Press, 1969), 142, declares: "The Wagner Mann loves is the composer of *Tristan*, in which the erotic intoxication of the senses enters into a 'demonic' alliance with death." Batts, in "Tristan and Isolde in Modern Literature," 84, maintains: "In this world the relationship between love and death, which was so often stressed by the Romantics ... assumes a position of primary importance. . . . The ultimate goal remains death ... the passive love-death through which they [the protagonists] will again become one with the universal will, Wagner's nirvana, the realm of night and love, the home of perfect because undifferentiated love." Gerhard Schulz, "Liebestod", 120 speaks in terms of "the consummation of love in death" and remarks that in Wagner's work "Tristan and Isolde have fallen in love in the sign of death ... their love was born, connected with death from the very start" and he enumerates this persuasively with an account of slayings, lethal wounds, etc.

[20] Schulz, "Liebestod", 127 uses the term "psychogenic suicide."

The marked kinship of the opening motif of longing to the closing melody of the "Liebestod" via transformation and expansion of elements which are quite similar in contour, can be demonstrated musically.[21] This undergirds acoustically the intimate correlation of Melos with the realms of Eros and Thanatos in this work. Because of such consummate artistry and economy of technique, the abbreviated title *Tristan* could serve as a shorthand cipher for the entire music-love-death complex.[22]

An important additional aspect of the confluence of Melos-Eros-Thanatos was the direct link of music and disease. This had been introduced by the romantic writer E.T.A. Hoffmann as early as 1817 when, in the story of *Rat Krespel (Councilman Krespel)*, he portrayed a situation in which music-making and love-making actually prove hazardous to the health and physical well-being of one of the partners.[23] Antonia, the daughter of the eccentric Councilor, an amateur violinist, is a singer who possesses a remarkably timbred voice of

---

[21] Bernstein, *The Unanswered Question*, 237, speaks of the transformations undergone by the famous opening phrase of the overture and demonstrates musically how "the final Liebestod" is already present "in nucleus form" in the initial bars of the music, which leads him to cite T.S. Eliot's dictum: "In my end is my beginning." For an up-to-date and provocative interpretation of the significance of Wagner's *Tristan* for *Doktor Faustus*, see Reinhardt, "Thomas Mann's *Doctor Faustus*," 111-12; 119-21.

[22] Reinhardt, "Thomas Mann's *Doctor Faustus*," using the typescript of the novel in the Thomas Mann-Archiv in Zurich and the *Thomas Mann Notizen*, ed. Hans Wysling, *Euphorion*, Beiheft 5 (1973): 61-63, points to a number of passages alluding to *Tristan* that were deleted by the author from the original text of the novel, in which this specific Wagnerian music drama played a more dominant role than in the final published version. For instance, in the original it is, significantly, Kretzschmar, Leverkühn's first music teacher, who introduces his pupil to Wagner via the *Tristan* chord F-B-D$^#$-G$^#$, the " 'chords of chords, this miraculous find of melancholically restrained harmony, so extraordinary that its like may perhaps not be found in music' "(112), this "quintessence of ambiguity as it 'hovers between A minor and E-flat minor in the third measure of its [the music drama's] prelude.' " (120) Reinhardt conjectures that Mann may have deleted so much Tristaniana material in order to conceal his actual fascination for this particular Wagnerian work or, in the final analysis, to pave the way for a greater role for *Parsifal* (121).

[23] An account of Mann's indebtedness to Hoffmann can be found in Dagmar von Gersdorff, *Thomas Mann und E.T.A. Hoffmann. Die Funktion des Künstlers und der Kunst in den Romanen 'Doktor Faustus' und 'Lebens-Ansichten des Katers Murr,'* Europäische Hochschulschriften, Reihe 1: Deutsche Literatur und Germanistik, vol. 326 (Frankfurt: Lang, 1979). With reference to the interrelationship of love, death and music in this context see Susanne Asche, *Die Liebe, der Tod und das Ich im Spiegel der Kunst. Die Funktion des Weiblichen in Schriften der Frühromantik und im erzählerischen Werk E.T.A. Hoffmanns*, Hochschulschriften, Literaturwissenschaften, vol. 69 (Königstein: Hain, 1985).

ethereal quality. However, since this unique vocal color palette actually stems from a physical defect in her chest, Antonia must refrain from song. She succeeds in this endeavor, until Krespel in a dream-vision discovers his daughter locked in the embrace of her composer-beloved, singing the soaring — and hence life-threatening — melodies which the musician had written for her. Upon awakening, Krespel rushes to Antonia's room, only to find her dead.

It was a literary-musical panorama such as that sketched above which furnished the background for Thomas Mann's early novella *Tristan* (1903). The title might suggest the portrayal of a love-death similar in magnitude to the tragic plight of Gottfried's or Wagner's lovers. But already after perusing a few pages of the story, one realizes that a different, much less lofty melodic-erotic-thanatotic relationship obtains here. The protagonist, Detlev Spinell, a second-rate writer with a first-rate ego, plays a wretched Tristan to Gabriele Eckhof-Klöterjahn's reluctant Isolde. Her boorish, all-business husband, whose highly unmusical surname she had assumed, serves as a modern-day Marke, sometimes the foil, often the fool, but always a tower of strength in the harsh realities of the daily struggle for existence. In contrast to Klöterjahn's exemplary pragmatism stands Spinell's exaggerated Romanticism. Spinell transfigures Gabriele's pedestrian crocheting and gossiping with her circle of friends into an idealized fairy-tale setting, with a crowned princess and her entourage engaged in song. Similarly in need of a corrective is Spinell's assumption that Gabriele was torn against her will by her crude husband from this bucolic surrounding of her youth, a milieu in which she frequently played the piano accompaniment for her father's violin. This activity is now forbidden her due to her precarious health following the birth of a robust infant son, an offspring who exudes the same vibrant lust for life as her husband. Gabriele is presently a patient at the sanatorium in which Spinell, still in good health and in no apparent need of medical treatment, whiles away his time.

The piano in the conversation room of the sanatorium becomes the focal point of the ensuing encounter between this poor excuse for a Tristan and the moribund Isolde, as seen through the eyes of the author known as "the ironic German."[24] Gabriele and Spinell are nonparticipants in the winter sleigh party arranged for the patients. As darkness begins to fall, Gabriele, who had excused herself because of migraines (a condition which, in Mann's works, is closely allied with the artistic individual), meets Spinell. The latter, a nonmusician, requests that she play "a few trifling little chords,"[25] and when

---

[24] Erich Heller, *The Ironic German* (London: Secker & Warburg, 1958).

[25] The English translation for *Tristan* and for *Death in Venice* which follows is from *Death in Venice and Other Stories*, trans. David Luke (Toronto: Bantam Books, 1988), 114/VIII 241.

15

she counters with evasive excuses, he draws out his trump card. Finding the score to some Chopin nocturnes on the piano, Spinell coerces the demurring Gabriele — he virtually browbeats her verbally — to perform: "If you are afraid it will do you harm, dear madam, then let the beauty that might come to life under your fingers remain dead and mute" (115/VIII 242). An ominous note is sounded, however, when Gabriele coughs as she reluctantly attempts one selection. But after some further hesitant probings, she gains full control of the keyboard and "Under her hands the melody sang forth its uttermost sweetness." (115/VIII 243) Spinell's words "dead and mute" portend dire consequences. The same could be said of his allusion to the melody's "uttermost sweetness." Yet Spinell, elated by what his prodding has accomplished, remains oblivious to the bluish vein protruding from Gabriele's temple as she performs several nocturnes.

The musical selection here, the Chopin Nocturne Op. 27, is noteworthy for several reasons, not the least of which is a corresponding passage in *Doctor Faustus*. The lush, romantic spectrum of sound associated with Chopin's emotionally charged nocturnal music is followed, in the novella, by the progression to the even darker sonorities of the *Tristan* score (the binding of which is, indicatively, black). The sequence finds a parallel in Adrian Leverkühn's major erotic experience, his fascination for the prostitute Hetæra Esmeralda in the Leipzig brothel. Adrian, somewhat surprisingly, follows his report of this erotic encounter with a commentary on music, specifically the romantic music of Chopin. He notes:

> But there are quite a few things in Chopin which, not only harmonically but also in a general, psychological sense more than anticipate Wagner, indeed surpass him. Take the C-sharp minor Nocturne Op. 27, No. 1, and the duet that begins after the enharmonic change from C-sharp minor to D-flat major. That surpasses in despairing beauty of sound all the *Tristan* orgies — even in the intimate medium of the piano, though not as a grand battle of voluptuosity.... (143/VI 192)

It should be noted, however, that there is an intrinsic logic to this sequence: the nocturnes stress only the music-erotic, while Wagner's *Tristan* augments this diad by an indispensable dimension of the triad: the thanatotic.[26]

---

[26] Another subtle link between the Chopin "Nocturnes" - especially the one identified as Nr. 2 in E♭ - and the music of *Tristan und Isolde* is the presence in both of a musical "turn" at key intervals. Whereas in Chopin's ostensibly nonprogrammatic piano piece this device still functions as somewhat of an embellishment, it becomes, in Wagner's scoring, an integral

No sooner has Spinell thumbed through a few pages of the dusty *Tristan* score, when there begins a series of authorial debunking tactics which undercut and thus undermine the otherwise serious ambience of this moment. For instance, Gabriele is struck by Spinell's quivering silence when he notes what work it is that he holds in his hand. She poses the very natural — but unanswered — question: How did this music get here? Then she sight-reads her way through the ambiguous tonalities and modalities of the melodic transformations in the "Prelude," adapting herself with amazing skill to the intricacies of a piano reduction of the orchestral parts. A third party present in the room, suffering from a combination of utter boredom and physical nausea due to this welter of sound, takes abrupt leave. The candlelight is extinguished and the music of Act II announces the advent of a mystical, all-embracing night (an intensification of Chopin's "nocturnal" music of before): "O sink hernieder, Nacht der Liebe." Again Gabriele asks a very pedestrian — and once more unanswered — question: What does all this mean? Finally, in the wake of Spinell's confession that he can understand music but cannot play any instrument, Gabriele launches into the third selection from the Wagner score. This is the sonorous "Love-Death" scene, in which the lovers, freed from the fetters of day and the burdens of waking life, are transported through their nocturnal embrace to a realm beyond the conventions of good and evil: "And thus they sang their mysterious duo, sang of their nameless hope, their death-in-love, their union unending, lost forever in the embrace of night's magic kingdom" (118/VIII 346). At this critical juncture the ecstatic spell is once again broken by the ghostlike appearance of a moribund guest who bursts inadvertently into the room. Even the climactic finale of the music drama, Isolde's self-inflicted "Liebestod," does not go unscathed, for as the final chord fades into silence, the tinkling of sleigh bells announces the return of the sanatorium patients.

Throughout the entire *Tristan* rendition, the hermetically sealed sphere of the medieval-modern lovers had been systematically violated by both internal and external forces. As a result, the full impact of the Melos-Eros-Thanatos experience in Wagner's work is filtered down to the reader in a very refracted form, a maligned torso, befitting the totally miscast Tristan. Just as the word "spinel" denotes a semiprecious gem which resembles a diamond but which proves to be intrinsically of lesser value, so does Spinell represent a sham artist and a poor excuse for a lover of the stature of either his medieval or modern musical prototype. Even when he indulges in "his" medium, the spoken word,

component - virtually the central figure - of the passionate love music of Act II and of Isolde's "Liebestod" and transfiguration in Act III, "Mild und leise." See Richard Wagner, *Tristan und Isolde: Complete Orchestral Score* (New York: Dover, 1973), 413 ff and 633-55.

he falls far short of the mark. His letter to Gabriele's husband is tainted by musico-thanatotic misapprehension and miscalculation: "An old family, already grown too weary and too noble for life ... and its last utterances were sounds of music: a few violin notes, full of the sad insight which is ripeness for death ..." (124/VIII 351). There is even a touch of unwitting self-incrimination in his accusation that it was Klöterjahn who put his death-marked beauty into the service of a shallow mediocrity. Given Spinell's failure to recognize the telltale signs of Gabriele's faltering stamina due to the rigors of the *Tristan* performance (especially the bluish vein protruding from her forehead more than ever), did he not commit a similar — or even graver — infraction against the sanctity of her person?

Not only does Spinell prove to be an inept correspondent, but he becomes virtually inarticulate in the confrontation with the enraged Klöterjahn. When, in the midst of this verbal duel of anti-heroes, news of Gabriele's imminent demise arrives, the spouse and would-be suitor behave in predictable fashion. Klöterjahn scurries off shaken, but denying the truth, while Spinell retreats to the hermetically sealed isolation of his room. The report of Gabriele's final moments contains faint echoes of Isolde's psychogenic suicide as the latter expires over the body of her fallen beloved: "[Gabriele] was sitting up quite quietly in her bed humming a little snatch of music to herself ..." (130/VIII 357). Even though the precise identity of the melodic fragment is left in limbo,. it is obviously an excerpt from Wagner's *Tristan*, perhaps the same motif of yearning which Spinell hums just prior to his encounter with Klöterjahn and son: "a little snatch of music ... , a brief phrase, a few anguished, plaintively rising notes: the *Sehnsucht* motif ..." (131/VIII 358). This potentially redeeming feature is then immediately relativized when Spinell retreats inwardly before the onslaught of the vital, young Klöterjahn. As a latter-day replica of the medieval knight and his Wagnerian counterpart, Spinell, tail between his legs, surrenders unconditionally; as a Tristan he has certainly cut a "triste" figure.

Although the novella *Tristan* incorporates many strands of the Melos-Eros-Thanatos configuration as it had come down from Greek antiquity (Orpheus), from the medieval troubadours or the romantic age (especially from Hoffmann to Wagner), there is little evidence in it of that magical ambience about which Mann wrote in another context when speaking of a poem by August von Platen:

> Death, beauty, love, eternity are the linguistic symbols of this both platonic and intoxicatingly musical miracle of the soul of which our poem ... seeks to make known in whispering fashion...
> 'Tristan' — is the title given it by Platen. How strange! (IX 270)

With Mann's own Tristan-Spinell cowering and caviling before Klöterjahn junior and senior, with Isolde-Gabriele passing ingloriously from the scene, living on at best as a faint memory in the melodic fragment from the more heroic past, the novella, written on the threshold of the twentieth century, bears witness to the fact that in modern literature the Melos-Eros-Thanatos concept was undergoing a drastic metamorphosis. Detlev Spinell contributed a lion's share to this radically altered perception, one which might be compared with the "loss of center" postulated by Hans Sedlmayr[27] for modern architecture — and by implication, for all the other arts as well.

Gabriele Eckhof's "unanswered question" concerning the Tristan score: how did this music get here? might be modified to read: how did this kind of music come into being? Just as Wagner's *Tristan und Isolde* inaugurated a radically new trend in music away from traditional tonality and paved the way for the demise of that harmonic "center" which had held sway for over three centuries, so Mann's *Tristan* stands as a milestone on the road leading from thought patterns of the past to the "disinherited mind" of the present.[28] The same might be maintained of Mann's *Death in Venice* (1911) with regard to its modifications of the Melos-Eros-Thanatos constellation. Here the modality of love is shifted to the form of homoerotic fascination. Gustav von Aschenbach, the author of classically disciplined prose essays, becomes enamored with a beautiful Polish boy whose name, like "liquid melody" and "exalted ... to music" (233/VIII 489), consists of "two melodious syllables that sounded something like 'Adgio' or still oftener 'Adgiu' ... with a long *u* at the end" (222/VIII 476). Different forms of music mark the various stages in the course of Aschenbach's growing fascination and infatuation, reaching an initial climax in the scene where an ensemble of street singers, "beggar virtuosi ... playing a mandolin, a guitar, a harmonica and a squeaking fiddle" accompany the "sweet falsetto notes in an ardent love duet" performed by members of their motley clan (247/VIII 506). Sitting within a few feet of the now idolized lad, Aschenbach listens as the mountebank, "cadaverous in the face" (249/VIII 507), sings an indecent ditty with a suggestive and lascivious laugh-refrain, at the conclusion of which the writer and Tadzio exchange knowing glances. Observing the frail youth Aschenbach speculates that he will "probably not live long" (251/VIII 511), at which point he recalls the hourglass at his parents' home many years ago, that "fragile symbolic little instrument" through the narrow aperture of which the "rust-red sand" had trickled (252/VIII 511). The

---

[27] *Verlust der Mitte: Die bildenden Künste des 19. und 20. Jahrhunderts als Symptom und Symbol der Zeit* (Salzburg: Müller, 148).

[28] Erich Heller, *The Disinherited Mind* (New York: Meridian, 1959).

confluence of music, love, and death in the above vignettes culminates in the frightening orgiastic dream sequence filled with a "compendium of noise," yells and screams, but "permeated and dominated by a terrible sweet ... flute music" (256/VIII 516). Aschenbach's nightmare scenes of death and destruction are accompanied by "deep, enticing flute music," and this comprises the prelude to the moment when his "soul savored the lascivious delirium of annihilation" (257/VIII 517). Certainly this scene of Dionysian frenzy marks a stage in the Melos-Eros-Thanatos linkage never attained before in literature and seldom, if ever, equaled in intensity (nevertheless, captured, to some extent, musically in Stravinsky's *Sacre du printemps*, which premiered a scant two years later in Paris).

The major tome of Thomas Mann that broaches the issues outlined above, however, is his late novel *Doctor Faustus*. In this mid-twentieth century *summa musicalogica*, Mann takes panoramic stock of most cultural values in Western civilization, and finds them wanting. Yet the tripartite configuration of Melos-Eros-Thanatos, although now radicalized and relativized to what appears at times to be the point of "no return," nevertheless remains intact. Not only is the music of Adrian Leverkühn composed "in a new key," as it were, but also his experiences in love and his death modulate to remote, but ultimately related tonalities. The tripartite formula, once compressed into Shakespeare's seemingly trivial and innocuous image from the opening lines of *Twelfth Night*, "If music be the food of love ..." now assumes new dimensions in the wake of such twentieth-century developments as the system of twelve-tone music, the revolution in sexual mores, and the holocaust of two world wars.[29]

---

[29] Schulz, "Liebestod," contends that the evolution of the "love in death" concept since the Enlightenment is an example of how secularized man has put himself into the center of the universe (once occupied by God). Schulz, 129, draws a very telling and chilling conclusion, however, and one which befits Mann's novel as well as Wagner's music drama: "We admire Wagner for his perception and articulation of the most profound conflict of enlightened, secularized, emancipated man. We shudder in the light of the realities of death in the twentieth century."

2 Melos-Eros-Thanatos in 'Doctor Faustus'

IN CHAPTER XXV OF *Doctor Faustus* we find the German composer, Adrian Leverkühn (1885-1940), sitting in a darkened room in the Italian village of Palestrina and immersed in Kierkegaard's essay on Mozart's *Don Giovanni*. Unexpectedly, he encounters in his room a real or imaginary figure, very protean in nature, with whom he engages in a prolonged and profound conversation focusing on love, music, and death. Kierkegaard's analysis of the opera and its emotional impact consists of three parts: an "Insignificant Introduction," followed by sections entitled "Immediate Stages of the Erotic" and "The Musical Erotic."[1] These same subdivisions provide a schematic framework for the major modalities of love which Leverkühn experiences, and therefore they will be deployed as guideposts for the discussion of this crucial phase of his musical career. This twenty-fifth and central chapter (literally and figuratively) in the novel, together with a myriad of minor incidents in the work, illustrate Thomas Mann's craft of fiction. They reveal the extent to which this author correlates even the smallest detail or motif with the grand design of his fictional composition. The polished craftsmanship of his prose together with the quasi-musical correspondences it engenders have been acknowledged and adumbrated so often, that this aspect of his oeuvre and technique constitutes a virtual commonplace or cliché in literary criticism.[2]

---

[1] Søren Kierkegaard, *Either/Or: A Fragment of Life*, vol. I, trans. David F. Swenson and Lillian Marvin Swenson (Princeton: Princeton University Press, 1949), 37-110. For an assessment of Kierkegaard's significance for *Faustus*, see Heinz Gockel, "Thomas Manns Faustus und Kierkegaards Don Juan," *Akten des 6. Internationalen Germanistenkongresses*, Part III (Berne: Lang, 1980), 68-75, and for an account of Mann's attitude toward Mozart, see Michael Mann, "Thomas Mann und Mozart" and Reinhart Zorn, "Versuch über Mozart. Zu Thomas Manns letzter Lektüre" in *Blätter der Thomas Mann Gesellschaft*, 16 (1977-1978): 5-8 and 9-20 respectively. The latter essay, 11, cites a footnote which Mann inserted into the book he was reading when he died, Alfred Einstein's biography of Mozart, in which he remarked that Platen's poem ["Tristan"] might be augmented here by the lines from "A Romance" by Edgar Allan Poe which read: "I could not love except where Death / Was mingling with Beauty's breath."

[2] See, for instance, Karlheinz Hasselbach, "Das Leitmotiv. Gebrauch von Sprachschichten und Sprachpartikeln in Thomas Manns *Doktor Faustus*," in *Sprache und Brauchtum. Bernhard Martin zum 90. Geburtstag*, ed. Reiner Hildebrandt and Hans Friebertshauser (Marburg: Elwert, 1980), 418-31, and Hans-Udo Dück, "Epische Symphonik in Thomas Manns *Doktor Faustus*," in *Vergleichen und verändern. Festschrift für Helmut Motekat*, ed. Albrecht Goetze and Günther Pflaum (Munich: Hueber, 1970), 243-58.

Whereas the role of music has been explored extensively in secondary literature in order to demonstrate the close-knit, "through-composed" nature of *Doctor Faustus*,[3] the reciprocity of this tonal art-form with the elements of love and death in the novel still remains unexamined. This chapter and the two following will attempt to show that the tripartite constellation of music, love, and death permeates the work from start to finish, from minor detail to major design, so that the isolation, identification, and interpretation of the smallest vignettes, scenes of more extensive proportions, and the overall plot pattern should yield insights into the structural essence as well as the thematic substance of the entire work.[4]

A. Insignificant Introduction

Just as is the case in Kierkegaard's *Don Juan* study, the term "insignificant" is used ironically in the present context, since the aim of the investigation is to demonstrate how significant apparently "insignificant" incidents and events actually can be in Mann's larger scheme of things. For instance, just after the narrator, Serenus Zeitblom, in *captatio benevolentiae* fashion, alerts the reader at the very outset to the shortcomings of his account because of discrepancies

---

[3] Agnes Schlee, *Wandlungen musikalischer Strukturen im Werke Thomas Manns. Vom Leitmotif zur Zwölftonreihe*, Europäische Hochschulschriften, Reihe 1, vol. 384 (Frankfurt am Main: Lang, 1981). Schlee discovers, in essence, an application of the twelve-tone (dodecaphonic) system to the thematic structure of the novel. Given Mann's self-acknowledged limitations with regard to the technical aspects of music, however, or his confession to Theodor Adorno that his own musical education hardly went beyond late-Romanticism (*Dichter über ihre Dichtungen: Thomas Mann*, III, 62), one might question the feasibility of such musico-literary correlations.

[4] Mann indicates in a letter of 1948 to Agnes Meyer (*Dichter über ihre Dichtungen*, III, 177), that what he was writing was "a novel of music, almost a musical novel, which sought to be what it dealt with. It is completely musical, composed with all the artistic techniques of counterpoint." It is the contention of this study that a prime contrapuntal texture of the work consists of the interplay of three dominant themes — music, love, and death. Mann maintains that while working on *Doctor Faustus* in 1943, he read pertinent sources in the musical and medical line: "Schönberg's theory of harmony and books concerning Venus-diseases." Interesting in this regard is the link, even in his background studies, of the tonal art and the erotic (in the radical form of sexually transmitted diseases). Another (1948) aperçu, in which he alludes to *Doctor Faustus* as "my Lübeck dance of death" (161), supplies the missing component in the Melos-Eros-Thanatos triad. In the same year, he defended the compositional methods of this work against a critic's harsh review by claiming — in terms which paraphrase the central idea of the novel itself cited earlier ("Relationship is everything") — that in such a work as this, "everything is connected to everything else" (177).

in temperament between the reporting subject and the reported object, he speculates:

> Whom had this man [Adrian Leverkühn] loved? Once a woman, perhaps. A child, at the last, it may be. A charming trifler and winner of hearts, whom then, probably just because he inclined to him, he sent away — to his death. (5-6/VI 13)

At this juncture, Serenus does not chide himself — as he is frequently wont to do — for committing a narrative blunder by revealing prematurely events which occur much later in time. Yet he actually does so unwittingly, by outlining *in nuce* the prime Melos-Eros-Thanatos components of Adrian's entire career: "this man," the musician-composer Leverkühn, loved heterosexually ("a woman, perhaps"), a-sexually or platonically ("A child, at the last") and homosexually ("A charming trifler and winner of hearts"). Whereas Serenus alludes to death only with regard to the last-mentioned liaison, he circumvents the fact that the second relationship also ended with the most terrible demise possible (the child in question dies of cerebral meningitis) and that a no less awful fate awaited the composer himself. What he deliberately obfuscates at this point in his biography, however, is that the allusion to a "woman" constitutes a reference with possible dual potential: positive and negative poles, if one proceeds according to conventional precepts of morality. It could refer either to Leverkühn's "pure" veneration for a lady from a salon in Zurich (the most likely scenario) or to his "impure" fascination for the prostitute in a Leipzig brothel. From the latter he contracts venereal disease, the fatal malady to which he eventually succumbs, but which also provides the catalyst for his greatest music.

At the close of the work, in the penultimate chapter over 600 pages after this initial allusion, Zeitblom recapitulates the above referents when recounting "the last years of my hero's rational existence, the two years 1929 and 1930, after the shipwreck of his marriage plans, the loss of his friend, the snatching away of the marvelous child ..." (482/VI 639). The casual reader may not recall at this point the original frame of reference at the outset. The careful student of literature, on the other hand — to appreciate Mann fully, one must be a kind of literary sleuth with a long retention span — should feel a tinge of *déjà entendu* at these words. Here is an important change in sequence marking the actual course of events in the plot, and also a clarification of purpose for the reader who immediately recognizes the identity of the figures in question. The "hero" had marriage plans for the "woman" (Marie Godeau); the "charming trifler" (Rudi Schwerdtfeger, the homosexual) who thwarted these plans, is remembered primarily as a "lost friend"; the pure embodiment of the "child"

23

in man (Nepomuk Schneidewein, whose pet name was "Echo") is now imbued with ethereal, almost divine qualities.

Perhaps even more interesting than what Serenus specifically includes in this recapitulation is what he deliberately excludes: the slightest hint of the two women who change Adrian's personal and musical career more than any other in the course of his life — Hetæra Esmeralda, the Leipzig prostitute, as well as Frau von Tolna, his ubiquitous but unseen benefactress. Thus we realize that Serenus Zeitblom carefully filters (if not censors) the account of his beloved yet bedeviled friend. Consequently, we must read, if not between the lines, then at least read the lines through very cautiously and *cum grano salis*, since the perspective of this pedantic biographer is all-too often at odds with the demonic and dynamic account he relates.[5]

Having traced with very broad brushstrokes the extreme parameters or the outer frame of the Melos-Eros-Thanatos complex in the novel in the two passages cited above, this chapter will now turn to specific events and situations woven into the fabric of the text which exemplify Mann's technique of variations on a theme. Subsection B of this chapter together with the entire following chapter derive their titles from the initial divisions in Kierkegaard's *Don Juan* essay cited at the outset: "Immediate Stages of the Erotic" and the "Musical Erotic." The two categories provide general material both diachronically and synchronically. At the same time, they trace and underscore certain constant features in the structure of the work which impart a sense of continuity to the fictional world of such multi-layered diversity.

---

[5] Serenus' problematic stance as narrator has drawn considerable critical attention: Margrit Henning, *Die Ich-Form und ihre Funktion in Thomas Manns 'Doktor Faustus' und in der deutschen Literatur der Gegenwart* (Tübingen: Niemeyer, 1966); Jacqueline Viswanthan, "Point of View and Unreliability in Brontë's *Wuthering Heights*, Conrad's *Under Western Eyes* and Mann's *Doktor Faustus*," *Orbis Litterarum*, 29 (1974): 24-60; E. Bond Johnson, "Self-Conscious Use of Narrative Point of View: Controlling Intelligence and Narrating Consciousness in *The Good Soldier* and *Doktor Faustus*," in *Literary Criticism and Psychology*, ed. Joseph P. Strelka (University Park, Pennsylvania: The Pennsylvania State University Press, 1976), 137-49; Volker Hage, "Vom Einsatz und Rückzug des fiktiven Ich-Erzählers. *Doktor Faustus*— Ein moderner Roman?" *Text und Kritik*, 50/51 (1976), Sonderband: *Thomas Mann*, 88-98; and William M. Honsa, Jr., "Parody and Narration in Thomas Mann's *Doctor Faustus*," in *Modern Critical Views: Thomas Mann*, ed. Harold Bloom (New York: Chelsea, 1986), 219-26.

B. Immediate Stages of the Erotic

After postulating the thesis that music alone has the power to seduce the listener through its "sensuous genius,"[6] Kierkegaard then proceeds to outline the "different forms assumed by the erotic in the different stages of the evolution of the world-consciousness."[7] The three stages which he proposes: 1. dreaming, 2. seeking, 3. desiring, do not necessarily correspond neatly to the three modes serving as sub-categories for the following discussion, which can be characterized, respectively, as: 1. maternal-mythical-emotional, 2. paternal-pedagogical-rational, and 3. heterosexual-homosexual [or bisexual] -a-sexual. These latter designations, however, have been derived inductively and intrinsically from a close reading of the novel itself. Such rubrics, although arbitrary in nature, do offer a convenient frame of reference to investigate the teleological progression of the Melos-Eros-Thanatos syndrome in the novel in this and subsequent chapters.

To illustrate what has been termed the maternal-mythical-emotional constellation, one need only cite the key role of women in introducing Leverkühn to music as a new tonal world. Included among the preliminary data concerning Adrian's childhood in the rustic surroundings of Buchel in Thuringia is a description of "the cow-girl Hanne, whose bosoms flapped as she walked and whose bare feet were always caked with dung" (23/VI 35). This rather earthy girl, "with whom little Adrian stood on a friendly footing because she loved to sing and used to do little exercises with us children" (27/VI 41), functions as the composer's first music teacher instead of his mother, as one might expect. Serenus is careful to note that the latter, in spite of her warm mezzo-soprano voice, refrained from singing out of a kind of "chaste reserve"(27/VI 41), whereas

> this creature [Hanne] smelling of her animals made free with it [song], and sang to us lustily.... She had a strident voice, but a good ear; and she sang all sorts of popular tunes, songs of the army and the street; they were mostly gruesome or mawkish.... (27/VI 41)

The casual comment about Mother Leverkühn's abstinence from music constituting a form of "chaste reserve" goes unclarified in the text, but should not go unchallenged by the reader. Does singing somehow imply contact with something impure? Can one pinpoint in a seductively "unchaste" Hanne a

---

[6] Kierkegaard, *Either/Or*, 51, "if this sensuous-erotic genius demands expression in all its immediacy, . . . it can only be expressed in music."

[7] Kierkegaard, *Either/Or*, 49.

touch of that "cow warmth" (68/VI 94) and sentimentality ("mawkish"), which Adrian quite emphatically rejects in music initially, but which he ultimately comes to espouse in his own late compositions? The erotic (one might even say erogenous) quality of Hanne is underscored not only by her physical appearance (flapping bosoms and bare feet) but also by the manner in which her voice, strident though it may be, insinuates itself into the singing of the three male members of the quartet: "When we sang with her, she accompanied us in thirds, and from there went down to the lower fifth and lower sixth and left us in the treble, while she ostentatiously and predominantly sang the second" (27/VI 41-42). Even Hanne's smile during the performance has something animalistically seductive about it — a feature which Serenus notes down, but notices only peripherally: "to fix our attention and make us properly value the harmonic enjoyment, she used to stretch her mouth and laugh just like Suso the dog ..." (27/VI 42).

Whereas the sensually explicit nature of this pre-adolescent music-making can be inferred rather readily, the whereabouts of any thanatotic component is a bit more obscure. However, it is subtly in evidence, being suggested by the content and type of the tunes performed by Hanne and her male cohorts. The subject matter of "popular songs, songs of the army and the street," aside from being mawkishly romantic, can become sexually explicit as well as quite macabre and gruesome, full of blood and gore, devastation and death. This is especially true in the case of street ballads, limericks, and military ditties. In this context one might also recall the "Moritat" or the "Cannon Song" from Brecht's *Three Penny Opera*.

If the above argument for a subliminal death component latent in this very early scene from the novel seems tenuous, then perhaps the appearance of another key concept in the immediate environs might help cement the presence of the thanatotic: the migraine headache. Just prior to the introduction of Hanne and her round-singing episode, we learn of Adrian's "tendency to migraine" which he inherited from his father (22/VI 34). This malady is frequently associated with the kind of mental strain to which an agile, artistic mind exposes itself. Yet later in the novel, the migraine becomes affiliated with both the terrible death of little Nepomuk due to spinal meningitis as well as with the syphilitic infection through which the spirochetes bacilli, by a process of osmosis, attack the cells of the brain. In the course of their migrations to the higher cranial regions, these invading forces of disease bring both flashes of exhilarating musical inspiration as well as protracted periods of excruciating pain, the precursor of dementia and death.

The purpose of this excursion into the headache-disease-death connection has been to illustrate the tacit presence of the Thanatos component early in the novel via the migraine motif. The latter is introduced at the same time that

Adrian has his first musical experiences (Melos) under the tutelage of the sensuous cow-maid Hanne (Eros). On an even more protracted scale, Serenus ties together beginning and end of his account by comparing the environment of Adrian's original Buchel home with the milieu of his adopted residence, the farm of the Schweigestill family at Pfeiffering in Upper Bavaria. Here Leverkühn spends the greater part of his later life and it is in this idyllic surrounding that his most daring compositions are born. Common topographical features of the Buchel-Pfeiffering landscapes (a pond and a hill) as well as parallels in personnel establish a "curious resemblance" between the two locations. Even though Serenus labels his premature correlation of the two locales a "strategic error," he nevertheless persists in supplying details of correspondence: "there was in ... Adrian's later home, and certainly not surprisingly, a stable-girl, with bosoms that shook as she ran and bare feet caked with dung; she looked as much like Hanne of Buchel as one stable girl does look like another ..." (27/VI 41). Yet there is one significant omission. No references to singing or other forms of musicianship are made, since by now Adrian has established himself as a composer of considerable reputation. But periodic allusions to "the barefoot girl" (204/VI 273) or to "her bare feet caked with dung" (256/VI 340) keep the original erotic frame of reference with Hanne alive in the reader's mind. In a similar manner, Mrs. Schweigestill's lengthy analysis of the "migraines," to which her husband is subject, underscores the Thanatos component. It recapitulates Adrian's hereditary headache and anticipates the affiliation of this malady with the miseries induced by the syphilis germs, surreptitiously yet relentlessly attacking Adrian's brain after 1906.

On three significant occasions throughout the novel, the figure of stable Hanne and her role in the musical-sexual development of Adrian are recalled. The first of these reinforcements can be found just prior to the time (1895) when Leverkühn enters the world of musical instruments and compositional experimentation in the shop of his Uncle Nikolaus in Kaisersaschern. Serenus interjects a remark on his friend's minimal exposure to musical stimuli up to then, noting "that it was by our singing of rounds with the stable-girl that, so far as I know, Adrian was first brought into contact with the sphere of music" (31/VI 46). While Leverkühn's improvisation and experimentation on the piano are linked with the onset of puberty, the second occasion on which Hanne is recalled occurs prior to Adrian's sexually most startling experience: his meeting with the prostitute Hetæra Esmeralda at the Leipzig brothel (1905), an event which will give a radically new direction to his life and career. Learning of Leverkühn's decision to abandon the study of theology for that of music, Serenus reflects back on "our canon-singing with Hanne the stable-girl, under the linden tree" (138/VI 185).[8] He then introduces Adrian's letter containing a detailed account of his encounter with Hetæra. As will be discussed later, Adrian's compositions after this meeting certainly result in music "in a new key." The final and fullest recapitulation of this motif cluster is found near the close of the novel, following Leverkühn's complete mental breakdown, his pitiful relapse into second childhood, and his return to his mother and to his home at Buchel (1930-1940). Sensing, even in this demented condition, the spiritual bankruptcy implicit in the closing of the life cycle when his mother comes to fetch him, Adrian unsuccessfully attempts suicide in the Klammer Pond at the Schweigestills, confusing it with its counterpart, the Cow Trough at Buchel.[9] After arriving home, Adrian is again witness to his mother's "still melodious voice which all her life long she had refrained from song" (508/VI 673). In a very real sense, the caveat of her "chaste reserve" had been vindicated by the fate of a man whose hubris had taken him soaring to precarious heights on his "proud Icarus flight."[10] Serenus recounts how the obedient little boy, now in his second childhood, sits placidly under the old linden tree "on the round bench where once the loud-voiced stable-girl had

---

[8] The lime (or "linden") tree does have certain affiliations with death in Thomas Mann's work. One need only recall the scene in *Der Zauberberg* when Hans Castorp plays several records on the phonograph and is particularly impressed by Schubert's setting of "Am Brunnen vor dem Tore" from the *Winterreise*, in which the "Lindenbaum" grants "rest" to the weary wanderer. The key to this text by Wilhelm Müller is said to lie in the relationship of forbidden love and death. In the final scene of the novel we catch a glimpse of Castorp entering the battlefield of World War I and singing, as he falls to earth at some point and disappears from view, a stanza from the same song. On the other hand, the presence of this linden tree image at the outset of Leverkühn's career at the point when he was introduced to music through Hanne's canon-singing, and the reappearance of the lime after Adrian's active musical life has come to a close might also be interpreted as a sign of the continuity of all things, even as a kind of eternal recurrence. These attributes are embodied in such arboreal symbols as the Tree of Life or Yggdrasil, the mythical ash tree in Scandinavian folklore, the three roots of which bind together upper, middle, and lower worlds.

[9] The linking of water — especially in the form of concave containers such as ponds and lakes — with the female sexual principle is common (albeit problematic in nature) to both Freudian and Jungian symbolism (the psychoanalytic school and the mythological-archetypal approach). This can be inferred from the respective discussions of "water" in J.E. Cirlot, *A Dictionary of Symbols*, trans. Jack Sage (London: Routledge, 1971), 364-67, and *A Handbook of Critical Approaches to Literature* by Wilfred L. Guerin, Earle G. Labor, Lee Morgan, and John Willingham (New York: Harper & Row), 128 and 157 ff.

[10] The Freudian view of the acts of flying, dancing and riding "as symbols of sexual pleasure" (Guerin, et al, *A Handbook of Critical Approaches*, 128) may also be applicable to this Icarus-Faustus context.

taught us children how to sing canons" (508/VI 673). The terminal stages of that ravaging venereal infection have rendered the daring, avant-garde composer a docile infant who has returned to the maternal sphere to die (the womb-tomb affiliation). Obviously the unique amalgam of music and the erotic in Leverkühn's life engendered a demise many removes from the "death and transfiguration" experienced by such mythic and literary forebears as Orpheus or Ofterdingen.

The second "stage" of the musical erotic, one which Kierkegaard labels "seeking" and which here can be designated as the quest for, and question of, the paternal-pedagogical-rational principle, involves three interrelated subsections in the novel: 1. Observing in Father Johannes Leverkühn's Laboratory; 2. Experimenting in Uncle Nikolaus Leverkühn's Shop; and 3. Learning in Wendell Kretzschmar's Classroom. In each case, Adrian appears as an individual groping in ever wider concentric circles in search of himself and his calling in life.

It is not merely through the hereditary headache that Leverkühn's father transmits to his offspring elements of the Melos-Eros-Thanatos configuration which go on to mark and mar the career of his precocious son. Primarily it is Jonathan's experiments dabbling in ambiguous and ambivalent subjects which fascinate the lad. Foremost among these are the collections of exotic lepidoptera and sea creatures. Singled out from the former group is a species of clearwings known as Hetæra Esmeralda and the leaf butterfly. The first of these is characterized by a dark violet-rose spot on its wings which, when the butterfly is in flight, make it more closely resemble a flower petal blown by the wind than a living creature. The second has wings, the upper surface of which radiates a "triple chord of color" (14/VI 23), while the underside resembles the foliage in every detail. In both cases, the hallmark is a pervasive ambiguity in appearance. Unobtrusively, Serenus has woven into the fabric of his narrative the name and natural disposition of the prostitute from the Leipzig brothel subsequently dubbed Hetæra Esmeralda, the woman whose existence and essence radically alter the course of Leverkühn's life and his life's work.

The allusion to a triadic chord of color has smuggled a musical constituent into the context via synaesthesia. The "fantastic ambiguity" of this species of lepidoptera is then transferred to the father's sea shell collection, for we read that in medieval times certain shell forms served as "proper vessels for poisons and love potions" (16/VI 26). With this description, the reader is reminded of the medieval *Tristan* legend, in which confusion between a potion inducing love became a love-death or love-in-death symbol; the Eros and Thanatos components have supplemented Melos. The latter is undergirded by the account of Father Leverkühn's ventures into "visible music," whereby a cello bow, drawn across the edge of a piece of glass strewn with sand, causes the individual grains to cluster into symmetric figures and arabesques. The death element, perhaps suggested by the "sands of time" no longer flowing freely through the hourglass but becoming "fixed in time," also comes into play in Jonathan's "devouring drop" experiment. This procedure operates on the osmotic principle, a process which, later in the novel, also characterizes the march of the syphilitic bacilli. The bacteria proceed with dogged determination from the infected area of Leverkühn's body to his brain, where they wreak their final destruction, after having induced sporadic periods of illumination and inspiration, Not only as a hereditary force in Adrian's life, but also through his pseudo-scientific experiments, Jonathan Leverkühn becomes a decisive factor in laying the groundwork for the career and creativity of his talented son. At this early point in the text, however, the reader remains unaware of the full implications of what has been conveyed in what seems to be random fashion, but what actually proves to be a carefully calculated strategy and symmetry.

The atmosphere in the shop of Adrian's Uncle Nikolaus in Kaisersaschern, is, in a manner different from that of the parental environment, conducive to fostering the lad's musical interest and, concomitant with this, his growing awareness of the erotic and the thanatotic. After having prefaced the account of Adrian's exposure to this new milieu with the aforementioned reference to canon-singing with Hanne, Serenus next links increasing interest in the "phenomenon of music" (32/VI 47) with the advent of sexuality as well as with the headache:

> So far as I can see, even at that time and for years afterwards he gave it [music] no attention and kept concealed from himself that he had anything to do with the world of sound.... it was at about his fourteenth year, at the time of beginning puberty ... in the house of his uncle at Kaisersaschern, that he began of his own motion to experiment on the piano. And it was at this time that the inherited migraine began to give him bad days. (32/VI 47)

Nikolaus specializes in making violins, but his home and workshop are also filled with a variety of unique and exotic keyboard and stringed instruments. While expounding on the latter family, Serenus recalls parenthetically that the viola d'amore had always been his lifelong favorite. There is a touch of irony in Serenus' predilection for this instrument, the very name of which speaks of "love," given his own account of his pedestrian emotional life and the humdrum nature of his own marriage — a shortcoming more indicative of "love's labors lost." This, coincidentally, will later be the title of Adrian's only opera (ironically with a Shakespearean libretto by none other than Serenus!), and perhaps could serve as the motto of his own life as well. If the allusion to a viola d'amore exerts a kind of deflating effect on Eros in this context, the same might be said of the singling out of the xylophone from the other percussion instruments because it "seems made to conjure up a vision of a dance of skeletons" (42/VI 59). This light-hearted comment alters the timbre of the thanatotic from the terrible or tragic to the "light fantastic."

But if, at this time, Eros and Thanatos can still be treated with a touch of irony or levity, Melos itself is serious business. Even though Adrian, on the surface at least, remains cooly indifferent to the treasure of musical instruments, he still is a witness to the weekly chamber recitals at his uncle's home. In spite of the increasing incidence of migraines, he proves to be a musical autodidact of no mean proportions, teaching himself to master — and unmask — the cycle of subtle chord progressions in fifths while sitting at the harmonium. Serenus is a witness to Adrian's

> self-taught and secret exploration of the keyboard, the chord, the compass of tonality, the cycle of fifths, and how he, without knowledge of notes or fingering, used this harmonic basis to practice all sorts of modulations and to build up melodic pictures rhythmically undefined. (46/VI 65)

Of course, such an unmasking of musical relations and enharmonic interrelationships leads to the aforementioned concept: " 'Relationship is everything. And if you want to give it a more precise name, it is ambiguity' " (47/VI 66). This formulation harks back to the ambiguous characteristics of the lepidoptera, to the ambivalence of the vessels fashioned from sea creatures. But more importantly, this formula augurs the evolution of a style of composition in which emotional expressiveness is acknowledged as the concomitant of rational constructivism. This potential *coincidentia oppositorum* results from a heightened perception, the upshot of focusing on a subject or object not from a monolithic, but rather from a dialectic mind set. We have a foretaste of this later development when Serenus discovers behind Adrian's manifest indifference to music a budding passion for this art form (47/VI 67). This passion is fostered by one of the performers of the weekly chamber music group at Uncle Nikolaus' home, the American-born, local cathedral organist, Wendell Kretzschmar. This soloist, composer and sometime lecturer for the lay community on the theory and practice of the art of music, will become Adrian's cicerone in the world of composition.

Kretzschmar is introduced in a chapter devoted to his career as a composer and producer of the opera *The Marble Statue*, a fact which seems of only marginal interest, unless one recalls the plot of Eichendorff's novella of 1819 bearing the same title. The protagonist in this tale, after being subjected to the temptations of an alluring Frau Venus figure, is rescued through the intervention of a love of purer, more pristine nature. Hence a seemingly inconsequential detail, the title of Kretzschmar's successful stage work, introduces the erotic element in its polar forms — demonic and divine. It is therefore not without significance that Kretzschmar, while still engrossed on the score, entrusted scenes from this opera to Adrian for practice in orchestration, only to discover that, on one occasion at least, "the intuition of the apprentice" regarding the most suitable instrumentation for a central scene, won the day (150/VI 200).

Since the exact nature of the libretto for the opera *The Marble Statue* is left in limbo, an alternate interpretation is possible which opens other vistas on the Melos-Eros-Thanatos complex. Much later in his life, when the syphilis-induced migraines become excruciating, Adrian speaks at length to Serenus about Hans Christian Andersen's Little Sea Maid whom he comes to consider his sister in affliction (344/VI 457). This torment is linked with her infatuation for the dark-eyed prince, with whom she fell in love when his "marble statue" sank to the bottom of the sea. In order to win the affection of her idol, the foolish nixie subjects herself to the agony of acquiring human legs in place of her fish tail. Leverkühn had been admonished by his diabolic conversation partner in Italy not to discount the "pains which the little sea-maid, as from sharp knives, had in her beautiful human legs she got herself instead of her tail" (230/VI 308). But this warning came too late, for he had already run the risk of incurring a similar erotically induced affliction in return for a special reward of innovative musical inspiration. Adrian's ostensible rejection of her bargain ("it is much more soothing to know that after death one will be the foam on the sea, as Nature wills" [344/VI 457]) comes long after his own pact has been sealed "in his blood." It is entirely possible that, given the extensive and seminal symbolic role played by Andersen's fairy tale throughout the novel (especially 343-44/VI 456-58), that Kretzschmar's opera, *The Marble Statue*, was more heavily indebted to the Dane's somber tale than to Eichendorff's "happy ending" story.

But the conjecture that Eichendorff's *Marmorbild* may, indeed, have supplied the plot for the libretto seems to be supported by the fact that Kretzschmar fosters Adrian's interest in this romantic poet's lyric verse and its transcription into the "Lied." Note, for instance, the ominous undertone in the appendage to a description of perhaps the most famous setting of an Eichendorff poem:

> A jewel and miracle like Schumann's *Mondnacht*, with the lovely, delicate seconds in the accompaniment! Other Eichendorff compositions of the same master, like that piece invoking all the romantic perils and threats to the soul, which ends with the

uncanny moral warning: *"Hüte dich, sei wach und munter!"* (77/VI 106)

The unidentified "other" work by the "same master" is the poem "Zwielicht," which warns of the dangers of twilight, that threshold-time of transition, when what appeared harmless in the full radiance of day, can unveil its alter ego, its threatening countenance. Again one is reminded of Adrian's harmonic experimentation at the keyboard which reinforced the view that ambiguity ("Zweideutigkeit") held the answer to music's mystery. A glance at the etymology of terms such as "ambiguity," "ambivalence," and "equivocation" reveals that the prefixes "ambi" and "equi" imply a kind of semantic stalemate between contending meanings. Similarly, in the temporal sphere, "twi-light" is the transitional period when two modes of light — that of day and that of dusk — compete on equal footing with one another. Since clear-cut distinctions are difficult, if not impossible, to draw when daylight merges into darkness, the poem ends with a word of warning: "Watch out, be attentive and alert." This is the first of several curt, cryptic admonitions directed at Adrian in the novel, each of which is embedded in a musical context. The remaining exhortations to caution, which will be treated later in some detail, are, like the first, not heeded by him. In fact, he deliberately flouts them, just as he does Eichendorff's caveat here, by plunging further into those very "romantic dangers and threats to the soul." The latter include Mendelssohn's masterful setting of Heine's provocative love song "Auf Flügeln des Gesanges" (77/VI 106), Brahm's serious song treating death, "O Tod, wie bitter bist Du," and the *Winterreise* cycle by Schubert, that "always twilit genius, death-touched" (77/VI 106).

Kretzschmar's lectures on diverse musical subjects for the edification of the Kaisersaschern community, grotesquely punctuated by outbursts of stuttering and stammering at critical junctures, are spiced with elements of thanatotic and erotic inference.[11] For example, in his first talk on Beethoven's piano sonata Opus 111, Kretzschmar theorizes that the work with the mysteriously missing third movement utilizes unabashedly "dead" conventions in a manner which gives new dimensions of life to them: "In these forms, said the speaker, the subjective and the conventional assumed a new relationship, conditioned by death" (53/VI 73-74). Stuttering violently as he pronounces these last words, Kretzschmar attempts to clarify the odd assertion. He explains that, in the case

---

[11] Gunilla Bergsten, *Thomas Mann's 'Doctor Faustus,'* 57, alludes to summaries prepared by physician friends of Mann on the symptoms of syphilis. The latter include: "Vague speech — frequent unconscious slips of tongue, inability to pronounce difficult words." In his farewell address, Adrian experiences similar speech impediments, slurs and slips of the lip.

of the great artist, what is "objectively" given by "dead" convention not only modifies his outlook but is also modified by his domineering subjectivity. The result can be a work which attains the mythical, the collectively great and supernatural. Put in other terms, one might compare this creative situation with the act of love itself. Both participants experience a form of "death" in so far as they cease to exist as separate, individuated forms, and enter into an erotic union which is collectively greater than the sum of its constituent parts.

Kretzschmar's second lecture deals with the late compositions of Beethoven. The preceptor compares the "afflicted artist" (57/VI 80), working alone at night on the fugue of the "Credo" for the *Missa solemnis* and engaged in a "life-and-death struggle with all opposing hosts of counterpoint" (58/VI 81), with Christ, deserted by his disciples in his hour of need. Once again, death becomes a metaphor for those fossilized aspects of a genre or technique, here the fugue and contrapuntal texture, which must "perish" in order that the "master" might infuse new life's blood into an otherwise moribund art form. Through the intricacies of dialectical interplay, such coping with convention also places the reins of restraint on the arbitrariness of subjective innovation.

Having introduced the concept of death peripherally in his first lectures on music, Kretzschmar weaves the erotic component into the textual fabric of his concluding talks. In "Music for the Eye," for instance, the sheer beauty of a Mozartian score on the printed page is regarded as a source of auditory pleasure for a deaf person, who would have to derive enjoyment from merely scanning the patterns of the notes, The line "To hear with eyes belongs to love's fine wit" from Shakespeare's sonnet is cited to undergird the premise (60/VI 84). Kretzschmar's ensuing analysis of the emotional qualities of music as opposed to purely intellectual factors, ostensibly favors the latter, until the speaker makes the following observations:

> "But bound as she was to the world of sense, music must ever strive after the strongest, yes, the most seductive sensuous realization: she is a Kundry, who wills not what she does and flings soft arms of lust round the neck of the fool. Her most powerful realization for the senses she finds in orchestral music, where through the ear she seems to affect all the senses with her opiate wand.... Here, rightly, she was the penitent in the garb of the seductress." (61/VI 85)

At least three elements in the above quotation deserve elaboration in conjunction with the emerging Melos-Eros-Thanatos pattern. First of all, the identification of the seductress, Kundry, from Wagner's *Parsifal*, with music proper and with orchestral music in particular. Because the latter lacks any verbal (i.e., intellectual) guideposts, the inarticulately articulate tonal medium is left to its own sensuous devices, and these can be devastatingly seductive.[12] Secondly, the concept of Kundry as music personified, flinging "her soft arms of lust" around the neck of the innocent fool is noteworthy, not only because of its overtly sensuous allure which is striking in itself. Equally significant, however, is the fact that it is with this very same image that Adrian later affirms his decision to forsake the study of theology for that of composition with Kretzschmar: "to change his profession and fling himself into the arms of music" (129/VI 173). It is no small wonder that Kretzschmar's reaction to this step is, of course, likewise an embrace (140/VI 188). Interestingly enough Adrian's earlier use of circumlocution, "Polyhymnia" (82/VI 111), the Muse of Sacred Music, to mark his decision to pursue theology instead of music, deploys a term which, with its stress on the religious aspect, deflects attention from the secular and sensuous — at least momentarily. The third significant element in the above quotation involves the image of "the penitent in the garb of the seductress." On the one hand, this idea of ambivalence of identity through disguise recalls the duplicity of the leaf butterfly hetæra esmeralda. On the other hand, it prepares the reader for the equally ambiguous nature of the human counterpart and namesake of the lepidopteran creature, the prostitute Hetæra Esmeralda.

Kretzschmar's concluding lecture, the exact title of which remains unclear, focuses on a system of musical composition devised for the Pennsylvania religious communities of Ephrata and Snowhill by Johann Conrad Beissel. This form of hymn writing entails a pre-figured and somewhat mechanical system of master-servant relationship with regard to different melodic intervals and harmonies. In spite of a certain rigidity in Beissel's strictures for melodic sequences and harmonic patterns, published as a preface to this book of the *Turtle Dove* (a member of the family of fowl sacred to Venus),[13] his hymn music is said to evince a kind of "erotic symbolism" (64/VI 89). This trait is already indicated by the title of the preface to the collection, the *Turtle Dove*, since this avian creature is closely allied with the love goddess.

Adrian reacts in bemused fashion to Serenus' amazement at the paradox inherent in Beissel's musical *modus operandi*: the combination of melodic rigidity with rhythmic laxity restoring that "bovine warmth" which any pedantic or aesthetic "cooling off" (through adherence to a prescribed system) had achieved. This assessment, however, harks back to stable Hanne's rounds and

---

[12] In contrast to those who maintain that the language of music is too imprecise there are others who claim that it is all too precise.

[13] *The Encyclopedia Americana* (New York: Encyclopedia Americana, 1960), IX, 284.

canons, which balanced the prescriptive qualities of a fixed form with the exuberant emotion of the singer and the sentimental content of the songs (in, for instance, "O wie wohl ist mir am Abend"). But it likewise looks ahead to the paradoxical nature of Leverkühn's full-fledged compositional strategies which will entail an emotional-rational *coincidentia oppositorum*. In a similar vein of recapitulatory foreshadowing is Kretzschmar's comment that music "always does penance in advance for her retreat into the sensual" (68/VI 95). It has overtones of his earlier remark about music as Kundry, the "penitent in the garb of a seductress" and anticipates much of the spirit of Adrian's late works.

Kretzschmar's lectures antedate Adrian's hard-wrought decision, in 1905 at the age of twenty, to forsake the study of theology at the University of Halle for that of music. Adrian follows his mentor, this pedagogue who is truly the "personified conscience of the pupil" (180/VI 240), to Leipzig, in spite of nagging scruples about the propriety of throwing himself into the arms of music. Perhaps this is an outgrowth of that "chaste reserve" toward this art expressed by his mother in her reticence to sing. In addition, Adrian has reservations of his own: the thought of producing an epigonal music is anathema to him. But his reluctance also stems from a source which he paraphrases in erotic terms: his qualms about having to sacrifice a carefree bachelorhood for the state of matrimony. Writing in an antiquated idiom to Kretzschmar, Adrian recalls his "mygryms" (headaches) as a schoolboy due to "cold boredom"[14] with every single subject, and he now seems to anticipate something similar in the permanence of his new arrangement:

> "sith I no longer am a young bachelor springing from branch to branch but have married me with one plot and one profession, it has truly gone hevyli indeed with me.
>
>   In feith, ye will not believe that I hold myself too good for any profession. On the contrary, I am pitiful of that I make mine own, and ye may see in that an homage, a declaration of love for music, a special position towards her, that in her case I should feel quite too deeply pitiful." (130/VI 175)

---

[14] A number of studies of *Doctor Faustus* touch upon the function of coldness in the work: see, for instances, Hans Ulrich Engelmann, "Joseph Berglinger und Adrian Leverkühn oder: über die Wärme und über die Kälte," *Neue Zeitschrift für Musik* 124 (1963): 470-73, and Ivan Golik, "Die Kälte der Dekadenz. Zur Kritik des Modernismus im Schaffen Thomas Manns," *Weimarer Beiträge* 17, Nr. 3 (1971): 151-70.

The deployment of archaic linguistic idiom may enable him to distance himself intellectually somewhat from the monumental personal data he is recounting. However, the frame of reference Adrian utilizes (embrace, bachelorhood, marriage, declaration of love) clearly indicates that the deeper roots of this decision for composition lie firmly embedded in the emotional and erotic sphere.

Even the facets of a music career which he discounts and deprecates in order to become "engaged" ("vow" 132/VI 177 "Verlobung") to music as a composer, are couched in terms of undesirable emotional ties. A career as a virtuoso soloist is rejected out-of-hand, since he seeks no "love-affairs with the crowd" (131/VI 176). The prospect of becoming an orchestra conductor leaves him, the epitome of an unsocial recluse, literally and figuratively cold:

> This quality ... was the expression of a want of warmth, sympathy, love, and it was very much in question whether one could, lacking them, be a good artist, which after all and always means being a lover and beloved of the world. (132/VI 177)

Perhaps the crowning touch in this letter which wrestles with the pros and cons of a musical marriage contract comes when Adrian tells of a nagging inner voice which admonishes him (another in the series of "warnings" mentioned above): "*O homo fuge*" (132/VI). A carefully concealed pun enables Adrian to speak "with forked tongue," as it were, since the Latin verb ('fugare') supplying the base of the imperative form "flee," is the same stem from which the noun for the musical "fugue" (German *Fuge*) is derived.[15] So even Leverkühn's hypothetical attempt to flee from the arms of music out of fear or disenchantment (and undertaken when he was "with headake" 132/VI 178), turns out to be, via a verbal sleight-of-hand, an actual flight to music's embrace. The very language he used left him no viable option at all. Whether the ambivalent message is inadvertent or deliberate is itself left in limbo. It is, however, a residue from the original chapbook of Dr. Faustus, which Mann has obviously refurbished to suit his often ironical purposes. But due to this verbal duplicity, one can point to another mode of the *coincidentia oppositorum* condition here: just as Kundry appeared as both sorceress and penitent in one, so the conjectured escape from music contains the seeds of entrapment in the "fugal" admonition to flee.

---

[15] Friedrich Kluge, *Etymologisches Wörterbuch der deutschen Sprache*, revised by Walter Mitzka (Berlin: de Gruyter, 1963), 223.

Kretzschmar's reply to this letter is also in the form of a written response, which precludes that his usual faulty diction, due to a stammering speech pattern at moments of high emotional intensity, mar the message. The terminology with which he counters Adrian's qualms about forgoing theology for a career in music composition, retains the concepts of the fugue (Melos), of bachelorhood, engagement, marriage (Eros) and even of migraine (Thanatos) previously adumbrated by young Leverkühn:

> "You are already twenty, and you have still a good many tricks
> of the trade to get used to.... It is better to get a headache from
> exercises in canons, fugues, and counterpoint than from
> confuting the Kantian confutation of the evidence for the
> existence of God. Enough of your theological spinsterhood!
>
> 'Virginity is well, yet must to motherhood;
> Unear'd she is a soil unfructified for good.' "
> (135/VI 182)

The term "canon" calls to mind the wobbly-bosomed stable maid and her round songs, while the fugue, aside from the implications just treated, entails the more sophisticated and complex form of contrapuntal polyphony to which Adrian will now be exposed. The risk, of course, is perhaps a "headache," that persistent motif in the novel previously linked with intellectual innovation and daring (Adrian's father and his experiments). Subsequently it will be allied with risk-taking in less cerebral spheres of activity, the cost of which to one's mental and physical well-being, however, could likewise be very high.

Kretzschmar's verse quotation stems from the *Cherubic Wanderer* of 1657 by the mystic Angelus Silesius. This letter itself serves as a prelude to the major piece of correspondence in the novel, one which Adrian pens to Serenus in sixteenth-century German and which Zeitblom in his pedantically precise fashion, prefaces with another reference to Leverkühn's flinging himself "into the arms of music" (138/VI 184) — only on this occasion the metaphor is literarily as well as figuratively true.

Even the seemingly superficial details of this seminal document have deeper implications for the bonding of music, love, and death in *Doctor Faustus*. The date and inside address, for instance: "Friday after Purificationis 1905" and "In the Peterstraße" loom large when one looks at some of the components specified. "Friday," of course is the day sacred to the Germanic goddess Freyja, whose domain included love and fertility.[16] The stipulation "after Purification" (in Jewish law, the ceremonial purifying of the woman after childbirth; in Christianity, the purifying of the Virgin Mary) has to be read as situational irony, since Leverkühn's initiation into the realms of the Eros and Melos gives rise to the suspicion that in each, "purification" has been attained by "impure" means. From this time on, Adrian will be the "pure artist" by dint of the venereal infection he contracts after stalking his prey, Hetæra Esmeralda, the diseased prostitute from the Leipzig bordello. The "hunted hunter" finally locates the object of his quest in Preßburg in the Austro-Hungarian empire. By the same token, the reference to the "Peterstraße" has a veiled implication when taken in conjunction with Adrian's later addendum that his quarters here were in the vicinity of the Collegium Beatae Virginis. Had not Kretzschmar admonished him before he came to Leipzig, that "Virginity is well, yet must to motherhood"? The virginity which Adrian had, up to now, ostensibly guarded in his own life will soon exist as a topographical designation, merely as a street address. It is only after his sexual experience that Adrian is able to "give birth," so to speak, to produce compositions of radically new scope and character.[17] One final note concerning this heading of the confessional letter: the year is 1905 and Adrian, at the age of twenty, is on the threshold of adulthood and majority. His actual sexual intercourse with the prostitute (and hence, the venereal infection and the onset of syphilis) comes only in 1906. Into this time framework (1905-1906) fall such pivotal events in the modern arena of the arts as the inception of the Expressionist group known as "Die Brücke" in Dresden. The name "bridge" may be indicative of a crossing over from the stereotyped, academic forms of painting from the past to the innovative art works of the future. Even more pertinent for this study concentrating on the auditory rather than the visual arts, however, are the fundamental changes in outlook which began at this time in Arnold Schönberg's concept of orchestration and instrumentation. Following the still romantically lush mode of "Transfigured Night" (*Verklärte Nacht*, 1899) and the *Gurrelieder* (1901) come the slender contours of the First Chamber Symphony

---

[16] According to *The Oxford English Dictionary* (Oxford: Clarendon Press, 1933), III, 543, Friday is the day of the goddess Frig who, in turn, is equated with Venus, the Roman love deity. Kluge, *Etymologisches Wörterbuch*, 217, observes: "Die Gleichsetzung der gr.-röm. Liebesgöttin mit ahd. *Fria*, anord. *Frigg* ist sachlich berechtigt, denn deren Name ist urverwandt mit aind. priya 'Geliebte' (s. frei und freien)."

[17] Leverkühn's first major opus, *Meeresleuchten,* still bore the earmarks of the Impressionist style of Debussy and Ravel and therefore had to be relegated to the "root canal" type of composition (the artificial preservation of a mode of music which, like the dead tooth, has been put on a kind of artificial life-support system).

of 1906. Coincidentally, and by way of contrast, this was also the year in which Mahler's romantically tinged Eighth Symphony "of a thousand" appeared, utilizing excerpts from Goethe's *Faust*. In the United States, on the other hand, the American insurance mogul and avant-garde, "closet" composer, Charles Ives, likewise completed his "The Unanswered Question" in the same year — a strange composition, to be treated in Chapter IV of this study in conjunction with Leverkühn's last work.[18]

The city of Leipzig, to which Adrian had been attracted because of Kretzschmar, was not only a *centrum musicae* renowned for its Gewandhaus Orchestra and its trade fairs, but also for its wayward morals, as Adrian's references to the biblical Nineveh suggest (139/VI 186-87). The extent of Kretzschmar's involvement with, or instigation of, his student's experience in the house of prostitution in that city is not clear. While Adrian still lived in provincial Kaisersaschern he had already been exposed through Kretzschmar to the world which lay beyond these narrow confines:

> The moment of taking flight, when freedom dawns, when the school gate shuts behind us, the shell breaks, the chrysalis bursts, the world lies open — is it not the happiest, or the most exciting, certainly the most expectant in all our lives? Through his musical excursions with Wendell Kretzschmar to the larger near-by cities, Adrian had tasted the outer world a few times. (82/VI 112)

The inauguration of this flight to freedom has earmarks of the "proud Icarus" adventure from which Adrian ultimately falls, only to linger in a state of second childhood and spiritual darkness for the last ten years of his life. The "bursting of the pupa" is an image which stems from the lifecycle of the moth or butterfly, the latter particularly apropos because it relates back to Father Leverkühn's collection of lepidoptera and ahead to the flighty "human butterfly," Hetæra Esmeralda. When Serenus later ponders what Adrian had actually wanted to communicate to him in this letter, he uses the concept of a "breakthrough" (akin to the shell breaking, the chrysalis bursting) as a frame

---

[18] Bernstein in the lecture "Twentieth Century Crisis" in his series, *The Unanswered Question*, leans toward 1908 as the chronological line of demarcation between music of the past and that of the present (or future). In this regard, see especially 263-70 of Bernstein's text. Coincidentally, Ives's original version of "The Unanswered Question" also appeared in 1906 and it was in 1930 that he began revisions of the piece (Charles E. Ives, *The Unanswered Question for Trumpet, Flute Quartet and Strings*, critical edition by Paul C. Echols and Noel Zahler [New York: Peer, 1984], backside of front cover).

of reference. He regards this as the overturning of the long-standing coldness and the absolute reserve of Leverkühn who, to the best of Serenus' knowledge, had never doted on love, sex, or the flesh to any marked degree before:

> We had never come on it otherwise than through the medium of art and literature, with reference to the manifestations of passion in the intellectual sphere. At such times he spoke in an objectively knowledgeable way divorced from any personal element. Yet how could it have been absent in a being like him? That it was not there was evidence enough in his repetition of certain doctrines taken over from Kretzschmar on the not contemptible role of the sensual in art, and not only in art. (146/VI 195)

Serenus attributes Adrian's sporadic comments on the sexual aspects of music — remarks which betoken "a free, unforced contemplation of the world of fleshly desire" (146/VI 195) — to Kretzschmar's pedagogy. Yet the student certainly did not prove receptive to the concept of musical eroticism because it was imposed consciously from without, but rather because it harmonized with the conscience within. The formal study of music theory, of harmony and counterpoint with Kretzschmar is destined to lead from the intellectual to the sensual. This seemed as preordained as the suspect cicerone in Leipzig leading Adrian to the "lust-hell" of the bordello after having shown him the St. Thomas Church of Bach. The master of the fugue and the ambivalent message of the admonition "O homo fuge" again stand in a reciprocal relationship.

Whereas Serenus insists that the musical allusions in Adrian's letter from Leipzig telling of his encounter with the prostitute are intended to conceal rather than reveal the sensual-sexual which lies at its core, it might also be argued that the erotic and melodic spheres are forces of mutual reinforcement. They should be seen in terms of correlation rather than conflict. The nature of the verbal medium in literature is such that it presents ideas and events in temporal sequence, like the progression of a melody. Yet it can be the case that the author encourages the reader to interpret events as co-incidental, as a kind of simultaneous sounding of verbal signs in harmony. Mann in particular makes it incumbent upon the implied reader not only to fuse the elements in close proximity, but also to re-fuse (that is, by "refusing" to overlook) long-range parallelisms such as the musico-erotic-thanatotic linkages between the composer's mentors, stable Hanne and Wendell Kretzschmar, or the analogies between the alchemical experiments performed in Father Leverkühn's laboratory and in Adrian Leverkühn's laboratory of musical alchemy.[19]

---

[19] For one of the most comprehensive and convincing examinations of the mathematical and pseudo-scientific bases and background of this novel, see Rosemarie Puschmann, *Magisches Quadrat und Melancholie in Thomas Manns 'Doktor Faustus'. Von der musikalischen Struktur zum semantischen Beziehungsnetz* (Bielefeld: AMPAL, 1983).

3   The Musical Erotic: Variations on a Theme

CHAPTER II SET THE outermost parameters for the Melos-Eros-Thanatos constellation in the section "Insignificant Introduction" by tracing the narrator's assessment of the role of love for Adrian Leverkühn at the beginning and at the end of his life. In the segment "Immediate Stages of the Erotic" motifs and situations were isolated under the two rubrics: "maternal-mythical-emotional" and "paternal-pedagogical-rational," which treated incipient eroticism preliminary to any love-relationship having deeper or more intimate implications. The next two chapters turn to the examples of heterosexual, homosexual, and a-sexual modes of the erotic experienced by Leverkühn and examine in depth the musical-thanatotic coefficients of these encounters. The overall scope of the "musical erotic" under scrutiny here is very broad, running the gamut from incisive, major sexual adventures to vicarious minor escapades, from "deadly" serious episodes to almost silly liaisons.

Chapter III examines two relationships at the extreme ends of the erotic spectrum: at one pole stands the woman Adrian dubbed Hetæra Esmeralda, the "infernal female," who prostitutes herself, but who has the redeeming features of a "respectable prostitute." She is the only woman who actually touched Adrian and who was also touched by him. At the other end of the erotic polarity is the "touching" figure of a mysterious lady who adamantly refrained from any and all physical contact with Leverkühn: Frau von Tolna. In the novel itself, her essence is characterized as "the eternal feminine." The present chapter attempts to analyze the unique modality of Melos-Eros-Thanatos evolving in conjunction with each of these widely divergent figures. Finally, Chapter IV examines Leverkühn's principal compositions as musical correlatives for the wider social circle in Munich and for the specific interpersonal relationships — intimate and otherwise — which gave rise to them. Even when the focus shifts to love of the highest order, divine caritas, the prime emphasis still remains the interplay of modalities of love with music and death.

A.   The "Eternal Feminine" and the Infernal Female: Major and Minor Modes of the Erotic

The designations "major" and "minor" modes are used here in inverse, and, to a degree, reverse proportion to their usual denotations. Musically speaking, the non-technically oriented listener normally understands by the term "major," a scale and harmonic-melodic pattern conveying a positive sense of happiness, gaiety, majesty. The minor scale and its harmonic coordinates, on the other hand, suggest something somber, melancholy, and at times even diabolic or evil. By the same token, these concepts ("major" and "minor"), divorced from their musical context, can denote "principal" (or "largest") and "subordinate" ("or smallest") respectively.

The discussion here is built on the premise that both the "eternal feminine," a concept derived from the figure of Gretchen in Goethe's *Faust*, as well as the infernal female, a legacy of Romanticism, embody aspects of "major/minor" in the dual sense conveyed by these terms. Gretchen, for instance, appears as a sensual as well as a spiritual being, a terrestrial and celestial figure, and in each manifestation she becomes pivotal for Faust's redemption. Although from the standpoint of actual time "on stage" she plays only a minor role in the sprawling tragedy, in the grand design of Parts I and II Gretchen constitutes a major force in the course and quality of Faust's odyssey from sin to salvation. The same holds true for the two women in *Doctor Faustus* with whom Leverkühn comes into casual or vicarious contact (but in each case, "intimate" enough to affect his life and music): the prostitute Hetæra Esmeralda and her "alter ego" Frau von Tolna. One critic has even claimed that the two women are one and the same person, and this hypothesis, now exactly forty years old, still persists to this day and remains basically unchallenged.[1]

B. Hetæra Esmeralda: A Morpho and Its Musical Morphology

Adrian's account of his experience with Hetæra Esmeralda in the Leipzig house of prostitution begins and ends with a musical frame of reference. Adrian concludes his letter with a prophetic (or actually retrospective and recapitulative) commentary on those key works from the *Tristan* novella of over four decades earlier: the Chopin Nocturnes of Opus 27 and Wagner's music drama. The Wagnerian linkage of music, love, and death, which had already begun to tarnish in that earlier fictional context, is here subjected to further demontage:

---

[1]This conjecture, originally presented by Victor Oswald in his article "Thomas Mann's *Doctor Faustus*: The Enigma of Frau von Tolna," *The Germanic Review*, 23 (1948): 249-53, has not really been refuted by subsequent critics. Bergsten, as a matter of fact, in *Thomas Mann's 'Doctor Faustus'*, 67, n.170, labels it "an ingenious analysis." For additional perspectives on the Hungarian question, see the two essays by Oskar Seidlin, "Doktor Faustus reist nach Ungarn. Notiz zu Thomas Manns Altersroman," *Heinrich Mann Jahrbuch*, 1 (1983): 187-210, and "*Doktor Faustus*. The Hungarian Connection," *The German Quarterly*, 56 (1983): 594-607.

Take the C-sharp minor Nocturne Op. 27, No. 1, and the duet
that begins after the enharmonic change from C-sharp minor to
D-flat major. That surpasses in despairing beauty of sound all the
Tristan orgies — even in the intimate medium of the piano,
though not as a grand battle of voluptuosity; without the bull-
fight character of a theatrical mysticism robust in its corruption.
Take above all his ironic relation to tonality, his teasing way with
it, obscuring, ignoring, keeping it fluctuating, and mocking at
accidentals. (143/VI 192)

Such a passage in the context of *Doctor Faustus* is significant for at least three
reasons. First of all, it retracts or, to use a phrase more in keeping with this
novel, "takes back," the dominant role ascribed to *Tristan* in the early novella
by regarding Wagnerian theatricality from a new perspective. Secondly,
preference is given to the "tones without words" in the Chopin nocturne, in
which one level of ambivalence (the lack of a literary text to supply specific
meaning) is enhanced by the ambiguity of enharmonic chords and key-shifts
obscuring definitive tonality. Thus what seems to be C-sharp minor can be
suddenly and subtly unmasked as D-flat major, in analogy to the Hetæra
Esmeralda of the brothel. She, like the leaf butterfly which inspired her
designation, appears to constitute a lower form of life, but actually exhibits
redeeming human qualities. Of even greater significance, however, is the fact
that this woman becomes responsible for the ultimate revitalization of
Leverkühn's music, making possible his highest achievements in art. The third
aspect of this musical excerpt focuses on two issues: the "protesteth-too-much"
quality[2] on the part of Adrian with regard to this "*facetie* and farce" (144/VI
193) and on Serenus' misreading of the intent of the "music-critical aperçus"
(144/VI 193). Are the latter, as Serenus erroneously conjectures, meant merely
as "trimmings, wrappings, pretext, putting off" (144/VI 193), or are they clever
maneuvers calculated to reveal as well as conceal the underlying truth of the
situation?

Serenus' suspicion with regard to deeply erotic roots of the musical
frame of reference should already have been aroused by some of Leverkühn's
introductory comments in the same letter. Adrian's elation at having written
down "a whole stook of droll studies in canon and fugue" (140/VI 188) must
certainly have jarred a responsive chord in the biographer's memory:
specifically, stable Hanne's canons (which Serenus himself had underscored)
together with the duplicitous "*O homo fuge*" admonition. Likewise, Adrian's

---

[2]Reinhardt, "Thomas Mann's *Doctor Faustus*," 111.

rejection of the "unthinking division of counterpoint and harmony, sith they interact so intimately that one cannot teach them sunderlye but only in the whole, as music" (140/VI 188), stirs reminiscences of that *coincidentia oppositorum* which lies at the base of so many ambivalent phenomena in this novel. These range from ambiguous butterflies and sea shells to the appearance and essence of people as well as of the aesthetic artifact itself. Finally, Leverkühn's allusion to "playing dominoes with chords" (140/VI 188) has a significant precedent in Adrian's experimentation with chordal progressions at the harmonium in Uncle Nikolaus' shop, at the time when, according to Serenus, the onset of puberty and musical discovery went hand in hand.

After this musical overture, which Serenus considers a camouflage, but which could also be regarded as an exposé of the Melos-Eros connection, Leverkühn launches into his vivid account of the Leipzig bordello. Here, amid the carmine cheeks, spangled arms, transparent gauze costumes, he spots several familiar "butterfly species" — clad in scanty costumes. His immediate reaction to this unabashed sensuality is likewise a musical one:

> ... opposite me I see an open piano, a friend, I rush up to it ... and strike a chord or twain, standing up, I wot still what it was, because the harmonic problem was just in my mind, modulation from B major to C major, the brightening semitone step, as in the hermit's prayer in the finale of the *Freischütz*, at the entry of timpani, trumpets, and oboes on the six-four chord on G. (142/VI 190)

Leaving aside for the moment the prominence of the second inversion of the tonic chord in the key of C major which is built on the note "g" (and which will be treated later in connection with Adrian's last composition), this excerpt reveals a unique response to unadulterated sexuality. The idea of "going straight to the piano, as though that alone were his goal ... as though for refuge" (113/VI 152) has a forerunner in the fiction of the novel itself (as well as an historical precedent in Friedrich Nietzsche).[3] Adrian, who, up to this

---

[3]Nietzsche's account of his infamous visit to the Cologne bordello, reported by Paul Deussen, *Erinnerungen an Friedrich Nietzsche* (Leipzig: 1901), has elicited considerable critical attention from scholars dealing with the philosopher as well as with *Doctor Faustus*. For an incisive account from Mann's vantage point, note his comment in a letter to Hermann Hesse (*Dichter über ihre Dichtungen*, III, 59) concerning the nature of Nietzsche's illness. Mann insists that it was not epilepsy, as some maintained, but rather venereal disease: "He shared the fate of many artists and especially of strikingly many musicians (and, to a certain extent, one can certainly include him among these): his demise stemmed from a progressive paralysis, a

point, has led a hermitlike (one might almost say a "hermetically sealed") existence, comes face to face with the erotic in its most elemental form. His immediate recourse is to music — and not just to any music, but rather to the hermit's prayer from Weber's *Freischütz*. This work is usually regarded as the inaugurator of romantic opera in Germany and, coincidentally, it has at its core a pact with a diabolic force which assures the protagonist special privileges. But instead of warding off the threat of base sensuality through this invocation of the hermit's prayer, the music proves to be a source of attraction. The snub-nosed, almond-eyed, dark-skinned wench, an exotic Esmeralda if there ever was one, saunters up to the piano and grazes his cheek with her arm.

Adrian's hasty retreat from this "lust-hell" (145/VI 194) is followed, in seeming non-sequitur fashion, by reports of a Gewandhaus concert. the featured work is Schumann's Third Symphony, romantic music credited with having liberated this art form from its small-town provincialism. Of course, Adrian's musico-erotic encounter will also free him from the confines of a similarly restricted milieu. In addition, the citing of Schumann calls to mind the earlier discussion of the composer's setting of Eichendorff's poetry. Not only is the latter's "Mondnacht" (a kind of cosmic love lyric) inferred, but also his setting of "Zwielicht," those lines which warned of dangers and threats to one's spiritual well-being by the darker forces of life.[4] Such forces, indeed,

malady which is clearly and evidently of sexual origin. . . . Seen from the naturalistic-medical viewpoint — to be sure, a very limited perspective — Nietzsche's mental development is nothing other than the history of a paralyzing release and degeneration, — that is to say, of being driven out of the realm of highly gifted normalcy into the icy and grotesque spheres of fatal knowledge and moral isolation. . . ." See, in the same volume, 88-90, for some incisive excerpts from Mann's essay "Nietzsches Philosophie im Lichte unserer Erfahrung" and also in this context, Laurence M. Porter, "Syphilis as Muse in Thomas Mann's *Doktor Faustus*," in *Medicine and Literature*, ed. Enid Rhodes Peschel (New York: Neale Watson, 1980), 147-52.

[4]Schumann, along with Nietzsche, Beethoven, and Hugo Wolf, may have been one of those "diseased geniuses" who, according to Bergsten, 64-66, contributed to the Leverkühn montage. Schumann's Third Symphony has been given the descriptive title "Rhenish," and the Rhine River also evokes images of peril, associated with the treacherous waters near the Lorelei Rock. This saga, invented by Brentano and perpetuated by Heine and many others, tells of threats to one's physical well-being. Danger to one's spiritual essence, on the other hand, is a by-product of Wagner's *Ring* cycle and the golden treasures of the Rhine maidens which wreak such havoc. Interestingly enough, both the Schumann Third and Wagner's Rhine music for the *Ring* are in the key of E-flat which, due to its nomenclature in German ("Es") has ties to Hetæra Esmeralda's musical signature ("H—e—a—e—es"). Finally, Wagner's attitude toward the waters of the Rhine as the source of life might be correlated with the elemental, primordial female force encountered by Adrian in the person of the Leipzig prostitute and

dominated Schumann's own existence and have now invaded the reclusive domain of Adrian Leverkühn. Is it, therefore, any surprise that at this same moment, the budding composer confesses his infatuation for Chopin's music with its "sublime incest of his [the composer's] fantastically delicate and seductive art" (143/VI 192), remarks which preface that strong deprecation of the *Tristan* orgies cited earlier?

The emphatic rejection of *Tristan* might actually constitute a form of sublimated attraction for that seminal music drama, as well as for the force of Eros at its core. The power of erotic attraction is now concretely embodied in "the 'brown wench' ... who had come up to him at the piano and whom he called Esmeralda" (154/VI 204). Another opera title, *Salomé*, a sexually explicit work in its own right, heralds the next stage in the alliance of music with love and death. Having ascertained the whereabouts of Hetæra after she disappeared from the Leipzig bordello, Leverkühn uses the premiere of *Salomé* in Graz (1906) as the pretext for an extensive journey to Austro-Hungarian territories. Oddly enough, he and Kretzschmar had just seen the German premiere of the opera a few months earlier. However, good, gullible Serenus takes great pains to assure the reader that Adrian's interest in the work is exclusively professional and strictly musicological, that the sensuous dramatic element did not interest him at all. It would seem, however, that the narrator is again blindfolding himself to the truth, just as he had previously considered the musical references in the confessional letter to be mere tactical moves to detract attention from the overtly erotic account at its core. The subject of love and sex was something which always made the staid Serenus feel uncomfortable. What Serenus fails to take into account is that music and the erotic are intimately bound to each other and that to isolate one from the other would be casting asunder what is actually intended to be an indissoluble union.

The reference to *Salomé* opens and closes the account of how the "hunted hunter" stalked his prey to Pressburg (Pozsony in Hungarian, as the text notes significantly) after his return visit of 1906 failed to find her in her Leipzig haunts. *Salomé* allusions thus frame this crucial erotic episode in the novel, just as the stable Hanne configuration was cited to mark the beginning and the end of Adrian's creative life in music. The libretto by Oscar Wilde complements Richard Strauß' powerful musical setting of a morbidly consuming love-hate passion (another modality of the *coincidentia oppositorum*) of the female protagonist for Jokanaan. This opera-cipher thus provides a fitting "objective correlative" for the kind of distorted, even perverted mode of Melos-Eros-Thanatos that suits twentieth-century (or at least post-Baudelairean) taste

with her dominant role in infusing "new life" into his musical creativity.

and temperament. Such an outlook is akin to, and apropos for, Leverkühn's own erotic adventure with Hetæra.

Serenus observes that Adrian returns from his journey full of praise for "the powerful and striking opera" (156/VI 207). This comment paves the way for an account of the musical innovations which Adrian will henceforth incorporate into his own compositions following his very real (Hetæra) and vicarious (*Salomé*) contacts with the erotic in disturbed or diseased forms. Hetæra, it should be mentioned, had gone to Pressburg for unspecified hospital treatment. In order that the reader not overlook the imminent death factor linked with syphilis contracted by the composer, Zeitblom informs us that Adrian, due to a "local affection" (156/VI 208), sought the advice of two physicians. However, each of these doctors soon disqualified himself for very bizarre reasons. Following these two bungled attempts at securing medical assistance, Leverkühn abandoned his quest and then suffered a two-day long attack of migraine. Not too different, Serenus notes serenely and innocuously, from those experienced previously, except for the severity. The afterthought is an ominous and serious addendum.

The same degree of ironic naiveté persuades Serenus' reaction to Adrian's proposal to attend a concert featuring a late string quartet of Beethoven. When the humanist expresses his desire to hear the Lydian movement[5] of the A-minor quartet Opus 132, subtitled "Thanksgiving for Recovery" (159/VI 212), the composer replies with a veiled quotation from Gretchen's love song of the King of Thule. The message of Goethe's poem reads that an irrevocable commitment to the beloved has been made, that a pact signifying "until death do us part" is now sealed. But given the kind of relationship Adrian has entered into, he seems hardly in a position to express "thanksgiving for recovery;" just as his physicians "abandoned" him even before treatment, so it would appear that any hope for a cure has also been abandoned. But the "unto death do us part" sentiment prevails.

Serenus' unnerved response to Adrian's report of his liaison with Hetæra is punctuated with positive, wishful-thinking assessments as to exactly what kind of erotic relationship might have been involved here. He claims to detect a "trace of purifying love" (153/VI 204) and convinces himself "that something obtained here like a bond of love" (154/VI 206). But the reverse side of the coin is his fear that Adrian is now "a marked man, pierced by the arrow of fate" (153/VI 203). The dire consequences of this bold undertaking are "that

---

[5]The Lydian mode in the ethos of Greek philosophers such as Plato and Aristotle was, according to Gustave Reese, *Music in the Middle Ages* (New York, 1940), 44, "intimate and lascivious."

love and poison here once and for ever became a frightful unity of experience; the mythological unity embodied in the arrow" (154/VI 205-206).

Freudian interpreters would be quick to point out that the arrow mentioned in both above images becomes, in the mythic context of Amor's bow which delivers such wounds of love, also a phallic symbol. On the other hand, the beaker presented to the King of Thule by his beloved as a token of fidelity or those sea-shell vessels which served as goblets for love-death potions (recalled here in the "love and poison" reference) are, due to their concave shape, vaginal or female forms. But how does this imagery and its interpretation accord with the "trace of purifying love" (echos of "Purificationis") which Serenus postulates for the deportment of the prostitute or for the "bond of love" which he conceived for Adrian and Hetæra? In other words, are we simply confronted with the infernal female destined to drag Faustian man ever downward to destruction (the "Eva" syndrome) or is there also an eternal feminine aspect involved here, an inverse, spiritually uplifting force (the "Ave" counterpart)?

A partial answer to this question can be seen in the fact that Hetæra repeatedly warned Adrian about the dangers which her body bore (another instance of the motif of unheeded Eichendorffian "Hüte dich" or Faustian "O homo fuge" warnings mentioned above). It was not her doing that the hunted hunter deliberately sought his own undoing:

> The unhappy one warned him who asked of her, warned him away from "herself"; that meant an act of free elevation of soul above her pitiable physical existence, an act of human disassociation from it, an act of sympathy, an act — if the word be permitted me — of love. And, gracious heaven, was it not also love, or what was it, what madness, what deliberate, reckless tempting of God, what compulsion to comprise the punishment in the sin, finally what deep, deeply mysterious longing for dæmonic conception, for a deathly unchaining of chemical change in his nature was at work, that having been warned he despised the warning and insisted upon possession of this flesh? (155/VI 206)

In spite of Serenus' squeamishness in articulating details of this relationship, the reader gains the impression that this union of intellect and instinct was not without redeeming features, even in the narrator's prudish eyes. Hetæra attains the status of a "respectable prostitute" by doing the humanly admirable thing. Thus she joins ranks with a number of emancipated females of noble character in German literary history, such as Goethe's socially outcast "Bajadere" or the "lost women" of Romanticism, in whom perceptive writers and thinkers found edifying, even inspirational features.[6] This is certainly the case with Hetæra, who supplies the impetus for a new mode of musical creativity (and is literally "incorporated" into the melodic and compositional texture by an innovative technique). But she also remains the source of the disease which, according to Mann's credo, both makes and breaks the artist: "genius is a form of vital power deeply experienced in illness, creating out of illness, through illness creative" (355/VI 72), as the pithy, chiasmatic formulation of the hypothesis later in the novel phrases it.

To maintain, as Serenus does, that Adrian never forgot this woman who "gave him all the sweetness of her womanhood, to repay him for what he risked" (155/VI 206) is a case of unwitting irony through understatement. This is especially apparent when augmented by the codicil: "Es war dafür gesorgt, daß er sie nicht vergaß" (155/VI 206). The German is given here since the English translation — "She might thus know that he never forgot her" — does not quite capture the ironic flavor of the original. Of course, the reason Adrian will never forget the "sweetness of her womanhood" lies in the bitter consequences of this act. The syphilitic infection, when misdiagnosed and maltreated, becomes a source of years of suffering and death as well as of days, weeks and months of aesthetic inspiration and creation.

Yet there is another, more compelling, musical basis for the lifelong retention of Hetæra's memory (a virtual immortalization of her). Adrian makes selected letter symbols or ciphers from her name — "h-e-a-e-es" — an integral and intimate part of his subsequent compositions in the innovative new style, from the first to the last ("h" in the German system being the equivalent of our "b"-natural, whereas "es" is "e♭" in the German scale). This is a familiar device used by composers in the past, such as B-a-c-h, and one which Serenus, in somewhat self-gratulatory fashion and in a characteristically belabored exegesis, claims to have discovered on his own:

> her name — that which he gave her from the beginning — whispers magically, unheard by anyone but me, throughout his work. I may be taxed with vanity, but I cannot refrain from speaking here of the discovery which he one day silently confirmed.... Thus in my friend's musical fabric a five-to six note series, beginning with B and ending on E flat, with a shifting E

---

[6]For the most recent investigation of this topic, see Erika Tunner, "Sirene und Dirne. Chiffren der Dichterexistenz und der Poesie in Clemens Brentanos lyrischem Werk," *Recherches Germaniques*, 9 (1979): 141-59 and Marlies Janz, *Marmorbilder. Weiblichkeit und Tod bei Clemens Brentano und Hugo von Hofmannsthal* (Königstein/Ts.: Athenäum, 1986), 15-118.

and A between, is found strikingly often, a basic figure of peculiarly nostalgic character, which in differing harmonic and rhythmic garb, is given now to this part now to that, often in its inversion, as it were turned on its axis, so that while the intervals remain the same, the sequence of the notes is altered. (155/VI 207)

Written from an extraordinarily perceptive vantage point for a musical novice, this passage is nevertheless central for an understanding of the overall impact of the Melos-Eros-Thanatos configuration for the remainder of the novel. Consequently, the full implications of this description as well as of its later modifications and variations will be examined in synoptic form at this time, rather than piecemeal fashion as they occur throughout the rest of the narration.

Adrian wove the five-figured tone-cipher into the melodic substance (temporal sequence of tones in horizontal line) and harmonic substructure (tonal simultaneity as chords in vertical configuration) of his compositions from the tentative beginnings to the perfection of what became known as the "strict style" (in which there was no longer any free note but rather every tone had its prescribed place and function). The reference to the motif's "peculiarly nostalgic character" (German: "von eigentümlich schwermütigem Gepräge" VI 207) deserves closer scrutiny. The contours of the five-note pattern in at least one of its possible realizations bear a striking resemblance to (but is by no means identical with) the opening five-note phrase of the *Tristan* prelude. This motif, because of its predominantly melancholy mood, suggests longing, but in its structural features, it also prefigures the "Liebestod" theme in the final act. The ascending line of the first two notes of Hetæra's theme is akin to the opening sequence of *Tristan*, even though the interval of the upward skip is a fourth instead of a minor sixth. The third tone in Hetæra's theme (an A, which, incidentally, is the opening note in Wagner's prelude to the music drama) can be scored as an appogiatura or acciaccatura. The fourth and fifth, in descending fashion, constitute, because of the enharmonics of the tempered scale, exactly the same tones (E-E^b) which are found in notes three and four in Wagner's phrasing (E-D$^#$).

Even more startling is the fact that Hetæra's theme closely resembles that of the opening bars of Isolde's "Liebestod." The contours of both Hetæra's melancholy theme and that of yearning from *Tristan* (the music Adrian once deprecated because of its "orgiastic" qualities) can thus be correlated with one another as well as with the love-death melody as the following rhythmically synchronized designs reveal:[7]

The manner in which Leverkühn infuses the theme into the "harmonic and rhythmic garb" and scores it for various instruments and orchestral groups is not necessarily a strategy unique to Wagner, but certainly forms standard fare

[7]Richard Wagner, *Tristan und Isolde. Complete Orchestral Score* (New York: Dover, 1973), 7 (Prelude) and 633 ff. (Love-Death). Leonard Bernstein, "The Delights and Dangers of Ambiguity," 227-37, of *The Unanswered Question*, uncovers startling thematic similarities between Berlioz' music for *Roméo et Juliette* and Wagner's *Tristan und Isolde*, and even makes the daring pronouncement "that *Tristan and Isolde* is a giant metaphor of *Romeo and Juliet*," 227, thus linking together via musical permutations two works in which the love-death constellation is paramount.

Bernstein's lectures contain several other enticing parallels to Mann's novel. For instance, Bernstein speaks of the tritone, that unstable interval which was "so unsettled and unsettling that the early Church fathers declared it unacceptable and illegal, calling it *diabolus in musica* (the devil's music)," 243. If one looks very carefully at Hetæra's personalized tone row "h-e-a-e-es," one could very well treat the second "e" as a passing tone and by sustaining the a-es interval (A-E^b or A-D$^{\#}$) produce the diabolical tritone or "devil in music." The dialogue with the mysterious stranger in Italy stressed the close bonds between Hetæra and the devil and his cohorts:

Finally, in his analysis of "The Twentieth Century Crisis," Bernstein not only comes to grips with Theodor Adorno (Mann's acknowledged mentor in music), but also seeks to trace some antecedents of that dodecaphonic or twelve-tone serial technique which formed a cornerstone of Schönberg's compositional strategies and, as will be shown later, comprised the central focus of Leverkühn's *Dr. Fausti Weheklag*. Bernstein's list of works in which precedents for the twelve-tone row technique can be found includes some key musical ciphers in Mann's novel: Bach's *Well-Tempered Clavier* (Book I) in which the chromatic subject of the F-minor fugue encompasses nine of the twelve chromatic tones in its statement and, immediately following this, supplies the missing three in the fugal answer (291); an ominous passage from Mozart's *Don Giovanni* in which all twelve tones occur (291); the finale of Beethoven's Ninth Symphony preceding the vocal "Ode to Joy" section (293) and, as "one of the most famous pre-Schoenberg attempts at a twelve-tone row" (295), the opening bars of a work which, by its very title, should conjure up for the reader-listener a host of associations: the *Faust-Symphony* by Franz Liszt (295).

in the latter's technical repertoire. But Adrian's method does not necessarily look back in music history (Wagner), but rather ahead to the future (Schönberg). By means of inversion of the Hetæra sequence and by "turning it on its axis," the intervals remain the same but the sequence of notes is altered. Here we have evidence of one of the principal techniques for potential variations of the Schönbergian twelve-tone row or dodecaphonic technique: the crab or retrograde canon.[8]

As Serenus continues his analysis of the Hetæra motif (or theme), some additional implications and ramifications come to light:

> It occurs at first in the probably most beautiful of the thirteen Brentano songs composed in Leipzig, the heart-piercing lied: *"O lieb Mädel, wie schlecht bist du,"* which is permeated with it; but most particularly in the late work, where audacity and despair mingle in so unique a way, the *Weheklag of Dr. Faustus,* ... where the inclination shows even more strongly to use those intervals also in a simultaneous-harmonic combination. (155-156/VI 207)

First of all, one should note here that the two works mentioned, the Thirteen Brentano Songs (ca. 1906)[9] and the *Lamentation of Dr. Faustus* (1930), constitute the chronological parameters of Leverkühn's entire output in what

---

[8]Donald Jay Grout, *A History of Western Music* (New York: Norton, 1960), 163. But, as Grout notes, the retrograde canon is also a feature of older music, used by the Netherlands composers of the Renaissance, for example. For a detailed analysis of these phenomena, see Puschmann, *Magisches Quadrat*, 35-40.

[9]The novel itself contains no specific evidence for dating the Brentano song cycle. Harald Wehrmann in his recent investigation, *Thomas Manns 'Doktor Faustus'. Von den fiktiven Werken Adrian Leverkühns zur musikalischen Struktur des Romans* (Frankfurt am Main: Lang, 1988), 35, attributes the composition of the songs to the Leipzig period and dates them 1910. But later, 38-39, he in a sense contradicts himself by noting: "Thus it can be no accident that the Brentano songs, which originated immediately after the infection, stand in the 'diabolic' thirteenth position in his complete works . . . and one must deduce: the invention of composing with twelve tones has as a precondition the luetic infection." Whereas I can agree with Wehrmann's second premise, I cannot subscribe to the first. Mann's text never dates the composition, and if, indeed, they were composed only in 1910, why would Adrian have declared to Serenus in a discussion following the wedding of Ursel in that very year: "Do you know . . . when I came nearest to the 'strict style.'? . . . Once [Einmal] in the Brentano cycle . . ." (191/VI 255). The time frame of this reference does not seem to apply to the immediate present, but rather to a more remote point in the past ("Einmal" in the temporal sense of "es war einmal . . .").

becomes known as the "strict style." This is a method of composition in which a predetermined sequential pattern permeates and dominates a work to such an extent that no note seems to be "free" in the sense of occurring in non-essential or random fashion. The twenty-four year period between these compositions is intended, no doubt, to recall the duration of the pact of the original Dr. Faustus with the Devil. One might, therefore, conclude that only after intimate contact with Hetæra and the contraction of venereal disease is Leverkühn able to compose in the innovative "strict style." Although this mode of composition claims to be free of the trappings of convention and of the stereotypical and clichéed practices of the Classic-Romantic era, it does, ironically, introduce conventions and clichés of its own. One of its innate shortcomings appears already at this early date, but is acknowledged only much later by the composer: a five-to-six note motif is too limited in scope to produce a work of major dimensions.

This time period for Adrian's pioneering creative output (1906-1930) coincides closely with the advent age of avant-gard experimentation in the aesthetic media on a pan-European scale in general, as well as on the German scene in particular. This situation persisted until the condemnation of all forms of modernism as "degenerate art" under Hitler (a verdict which would definitely have applied to Adrian's music and led to its disappearance, if not destruction).

A second important aspect in Serenus' comments stems from the fact that Adrian composes his first works in the radically innovative format to poems by the German romantic poet, Clemens Brentano (1778-1842). Bretano had a reputation for literary innovation[10] as well as for bizarre, erotic escapades, running the gamut from street walkers to "poetesses of the body,"[11] from prudes and prostitutes to an astigmatized nun. This stereotypical view of Brentano has been well established in the annals of literary history,

---

[10]Hans Magnus Enzensberger, *Brentanos Poetik* (Munich: Hanser, 1961) for instance, in his controversial study, demonstrates the extent to which the poet can be regarded as one of the genuine forerunners of modernity.

[11]Clemens Brentano, *Godwi oder das steinerne Bild der Mutter*, in *Werke* vol. II, ed. Friedhelm Kemp (Munich: Hanser, 1963), 292.

both canonical and apocryphal.[12] Thus mere mention of the name "Brentano" could serve, at least for the educated German reading public, as a shorthand cipher for an artist, much of whose love-life is closely linked with the type of woman portrayed in his series of "songs of prostitutes."[13]

One of the most notorious of these is the poem "Die Welt war mir zuwider," every stanza of which concludes with the refrain specifically cited by Serenus: "O dear girl, how evil you are." The oxymoron in this verse ("dear — evil") underscores the third element of note here. This feature has already been referred to elsewhere as the *coincidentia oppositorum* principle, the coexistence in life and in art of attributes which normally tend to be mutually exclusive or which can, at best, complement each other. Hetæra is a "dear" person in so far as she remains admirably frank about her condition before granting Adrian "all the sweetness of womanhood." She tries her best to ward off his advances; in the paragraph portraying the clandestine Pressburg meeting, the words "warn" or "warning" occur no less than five times within a short period, But when this admonition goes unheeded, she acts sincerely in her surrender to the composer's demands. Yet in the eyes of a less discriminating public, she is and remains a force of "evil," not only because of what public opinion brands such "women of the night," but because she transmits to those who patronize her a debilitating and ultimately fatal malady. Of course, this attitude overlooks the "inspirational" factor which Thomas Mann, in his frequently idiosyncratic outlook on the origins of art, attributes to certain illnesses or psychic aberrations. In the description of Leverkühn's fatal attraction to Hetæra, Serenus had spoken of a "deep, deeply mysterious longing for dæmonic

---

[12]John Fetzer, "Nachklänge Brentanoscher Musik in Thomas Manns *Doktor Faustus*," *Clemens Brentano. Beiträge des Kolloquiums im Freien Deutschen Hochstift 1978*, ed. Detlev Lüders (Tübingen: Niemeyer, 1980), 33-46.

[13]During the years 1811-1812 Brentano seems to have produced a cluster of such poems: in addition to "Die Welt war mir zuwider," which contains the key refrain "O lieb Mädel, wie schlecht bist du!", one might also mention: "Wohlan! so bin ich deiner los/ Du freches lüderliches Weib!" and the ballad ironically known as "Treulieb." The infamously famous "Ich kenn ein Haus, ein Freudenhaus" stems from a somewhat later date. In this connection, see Karl Eibl, "Suche nach Wirklichkeit. Zur 'romantischen Ironie' in Clemens Brentanos Dirnengedichten," in *Romantik. Ein literaturwissenschaftliches Studienbuch*, ed. Ernst Ribbat (Königstein/Ts.: Athenäum, 1979), 98-113, and, most recently, Gabriele Brandstetter, *Erotik und Religiosität. Zur Lyrik Clemens Brentanos*, Münchner Germanistische Beiträge, vol. 33 (Munich: Fink, 1986), 52-103.

conception, for a deathly unchaining of chemical change in his nature." Because they disrupt the normal routine and prevent the infected organism from atrophying in the stultified pathways of life, such invasive maladies may grant the already talented or even "normal" host individual extraordinary powers and creative impulses. This can be only on a short term basis, however, and these bacilli claim their toll in the long run. Each of Adrian's compositions after his infection will embody the principle of the oxymoron or the coincidence of opposites first introduced musically and textually in the setting of the Brentano song about the dear-evil woman. But this attribute only reinforces a trait that had been latent in the "ambiguity" indigenous to music from the outset.

Subsequent information on the Brentano song cycle is interspersed throughout Adrian's theoretical discussions with Kretzschmar concerning the problems facing the twentieth-century composer. One of the most intense such exchanges of ideas focuses on three topics: the degree to which art feigns one state of mind while actually conveying another; the nature of the marriage bond between the verbal and tonal media in the musical scoring of lyric poetry; and the course of evolution for the "strict style" of composition.

With regard to the first of these subjects, the thirteen songs in the Brentano group are said to illustrate "at once a mockery and a glorification of the fundamental, a painfully reminiscent ironic treatment of tonality, of the tempered system, of traditional music itself" (182/VI 243). If a composer can simultaneously mock and glorify the fundamental tonal center or tonic key, is this not tantamount to the juxtaposition of features felt to be contradictory — a clear-cut musical counterpart to a poetic text about a "dear-evil" girl? The ironizing of tonality likewise incorporates a mode of musical ambi-valence or ambiguous potential akin to that originally conceived by Adrian at the harmonium in his uncle's shop and based on the enharmonic principle. According to this procedure, a note or chordal pattern can, by virtue of the tones it shares in common with a chord from a different key, function either in its intrinsic tonality or leap to a distantly related, but perfectly logical milieu. Does this musical dual potential not resemble the situation of a lowly, diseased prostitute who becomes the force behind the rise and demise of a musical pioneer of the twentieth century?

The establishment of the tempered system for tuning instruments is a necessary corollary to the enharmonic potential, since in the period prior to Bach's "well-tempered" clavichord, a note such as G sharp was not identical with A flat, but rather became so after the tempering process had been introduced. This was, at least, the case with the keyboard instruments or with others such as the woodwinds, the tuning mechanism of which was not as flexible as that of the strings or certain members of the brass family. This situation made possible the kind of tonal equivocation exploited by the practitioners of enharmonic change, a technique especially fostered by composers of the romantic persuasion (from Schubert and Schumann to Mahler). This parallels the dual perspective of the prostitute as both a destructive *femme fatale* and a constructive, catalytic impetus towards a better humanity and/or aesthetic creativity. Such a trend became widespread, common currency among romantic writers from Brentano to Baudelaire, and persisted to Mann's day in the mid-twentieth century with Jean-Paul Sartre's *La Putain respectueuse* (1946).

Serenus' analysis of the thirteen Brentano songs, "this lyric marrying of music with words" (182/VI 243), is couched in terms of love and death experiences.[14] Adrian's insistence that the songs not be performed in isolation or separately, but rather that the cycle be played only in its entirety, seems to suggest that music, love, and death comprise an inviolable tri-unity:

> Yet Leverkühn wanted them all regarded and treated together,
> as a whole, proceeding from one definite, fundamental stylistic
> conception, the congenial contact with a particular, amazingly
> lofty, and deeply dream-sunken poet soul. (182/VI 243)

Experiencing the impact of the full-range of this poetry and its musical transcription is akin to regarding the "dear-evil" prostitute Hetæra from an all-encompassing vantage point rather than monolithically, as the embodiment of unadulterated sensuality. It is only when the full panorama of her personality is taken into account, when the entire scope of the aesthetic-ethical spectrum is considered, that the full essence of either her humanity or the aesthetic artifact emerges. Characterizing the relationship of Brentano, the complex "modern" writer, to the folksong, Serenus speaks of a "cultural paradox which by inversion of the natural course of development, where the refined and intellectual grow out of the elementary, the former here plays the role of the

---

[14]Interestingly enough, Schulz, "Liebestod," 126, when speaking of Brentano's *Godwi*, claims that "in this novel the word 'Liebestod' seems to appear for the first time in the German language."

original, out of which the simple continually strives to wrest itself free" (183/VI 244-45).[15]

In order to illustrate the contention that " rarely in all literature have word and music met and married as here" (183/VI 245), Serenus cites a stanza from Brentano which "transposes" Adrian's musical dictum that "Relationship is everything" into a strictly romantic key:

All is so gently and friendly combining,
Hand seeketh hand in sympathy kind,
Lights through the night wind trusting, consoling,
All is in union for ever entwined. (183/VI 245)

Zeitblom concludes his initial commentary on the thirteen Brentano songs with a set of variations on his previous theme:

Very rarely in all literature have word and music met and married as here.... These notes, that consoling and trusting offer each other the hand; that weaving and winding of all things in likeness and change — of such it is, and Adrian Leverkühn is its youthful master. (183/VI 245)

The phrase "hand seeketh hand in sympathy kind," introduced unobtrusively by Brentano's verses and then taken up by the prose exegesis, will later recur in those human relationships in which the element of eroticism is superseded by that of a kind of altruism. This will be particularly true of those instances in which Eros cedes precedence to a love of an all-encompassing sort: Caritas.

In a subsequent discussion (1910) with Serenus concerning the evolution of a "strict style" as a phenomenon that breaks down those antinomous and autonomous barriers which then prove to be complementary rather than contradictory, Adrian amplifies what this term entails. "I will tell you" he says, "what I understand by 'strict style.' I mean the complete integration of all musical dimensions, their neutrality towards each other due to complete organization" (191/VI 255). It should be noted that this excursion into

---

[15]Walter Müller-Seidel's article "Brentanos naive und sentimentalische Poesie," *Jahrbuch der Deutschen Schillergesellschaft*, 18 (1974): 441-65, works with the familiar Schillerian dichotomy and comes to the conclusion (459) that the Romantic writer can be characterized as a "reflective poet of the naive."

composition follows on the heels of the marriage ceremony of Adrian's sister, on which occasion "he was suffering from headache" (186/VI 248). This "sacrificial feast of a maidenhead" (186/VI 248) is followed by a very frank probing of the nuptial vow that the "twain shall be one flesh" (187/VI 250). With the elements of Eros and Thanatos here in evidence, it is not surprising that on this occasion Adrian launches into his most detailed analysis of Melos. He maintains that the strict style, having once established itself on a tentative and limited basis, must now evolve on a more comprehensive scale:

> Do you know ... when I came nearest to the "strict style"? Once in the Brentano cycle ... in "*O lieb Mädel.*" That song is entirely derived from a fundamental figure, a series of interchangeable intervals, the five notes, B[H], E, A, E, E-flat, and the horizontal melody and the vertical harmony are determined and controlled by it, in so far as that is possible with a basic motif of so few notes. It is like a word, a key word, stamped on everything in the song, which it would like to determine entirely. But it is too short a word and in itself not flexible enough. The tonal space it affords is too limited. (191/VI 255)

By anticipating the expansion of the five-note motif to a full-fledged twelve-letter (or twelve-syllabic) verbal utterance, Leverkühn inadvertently outlines the schematic-thematic, Schönbergian design of this final work, the *Lamentation of Dr. Faustus*:

> One would have to go on from here and make longer words out of the twelve letters, as it were, of the tempered semitone alphabet. Words of twelve letters, certain combinations and interrelations of twelve semitones, series of notes from which a piece and all the movements of a work must strictly derive. Every note of the whole composition, both melody and harmony, would have to show its relation to this fixed fundamental series. Not one might recur until the other notes have sounded. Not one might appear which did not fulfill its function in the whole structure. There would no longer be a free note. That is what I would call "strict composition." (191/VI 255-56)

One must, first of all, take into account the context in which this dialogue is set — the "swindling the Devil out of the carnal concomitant and making a sacrament of it, the sacrament of Christian marriage" (186/VI 249). Secondly, one can ally this with earlier utterances such as the "marriage of music and the word," "all is in union for ever entwined," or with the reciprocity of instinct and intellect in the "dear-evil" Hetæra. Thirdly, one should consider the all-pervasive network of musical correspondences and correlations engendered by the strict style with its melodic-harmonic interdependencies and integration. Only at this point does one begin to gain some idea of the grandiose scale on which Mann applied Adrian's early watchword: "Relationship is everything" as well as its later revised formulation: "organization is everything" to the texture of the novel itself.

Three subsequent references to the Brentano song cycle and its Melos-Eros-Thanatos implications should be mentioned due to the incisive nature of these remarks. The first is found in Adrian's dialogue with his real or imagined "devil's" advocate in Italy. The latter, commenting on his own unstable, protean appearance, compares himself with the elusive leaf butterfly and claims to be "Esmeralda's friend and cohabitant" (233/VI 311). Then he alludes maliciously to Leverkühn's "pretty song with the letter symbol— oh, really ingeniously done, and almost as though by inspiration" (228/VI 304). This cynically tinged comment is supplemented by a further quotation from that same poem:

> When once thou gavest to me
> At night the cooling draught,
> With poison didst undo me (228/VI 305)

The image of a "cooling draught" which proves toxic, brings to mind not only the medieval sea shells from Father Jonathan's collection, which were used for both sacred and profane purposes, but also the love-death potion from *Tristan*. Clearly, in the context of the Brentano verses, the reference is patently to venereal infection. With tongue in cheek, Adrian's antagonist informs him that a Munich acquaintance of the composer, Baptist Spengler, is also an "Esmeraldus." This remark seems of only marginal consequence, until we later learn that this same individual, an otherwise boorish secessionist painter of mediocre talent who seeks sexual titillation in art, is inordinately interested in the Brentano songs. "The sexual interested him in a literary sense, sex and esprit lying with him very close together..." (259/VI 345). Spengler had purchased the score of the Brentano cycle, studied it at the piano, and thus feels qualified to pontificate provocatively on the cycle:

> He delivered himself at that time of the remark that occupation with these songs ended by spoiling one, quite definitely and almost dangerously. Afterwards one could hardly find pleasure in anything in that field.... Spoilt by the extraordinary, his taste ruined for anything else, he must at last deteriorate through despair of executing the impossible. (259/VI 345)

In spite of his avowed allegiance to innovative, anti-establishment art, Spengler is a man of limited aesthetic sensibilities. And yet even he detects in this new idiom something which threatened to destroy his appreciation for the conventions of the genre. There is here a precarious hovering on the razor's edge between possibility and impossibility. This may stem from the musical setting per se, from Brentano's poetry which gave rise to this setting, or from the lifestyles of the poet/composer, which enabled them to articulate existential dilemmas so persuasively. Even a combination of all three conjectures is not outside the realm of probability.

The third and final significant allusion to the Brentano cycle comes during the discussion of Adrian's crowning achievement *Dr. Fausti Weheklag* or *Lamentation of Doctor Faustus*. Leverkühn invites a group of friends and acquaintances to Pfeiffering in 1930, ostensibly to hear the premiere of his testament in music (ironically, he even invites Spengler, not realizing that the latter had long ago succumbed to his syphilitic malady). Adrian begins by laying bare his soul to the disquieted group with what for most of them must be cryptically encoded references:

> For it was but a butterfly, a bright cream-licker, Hetæra Esmeralda, she charmed me with her touch, the milk-witch, and I followed after her into the twilit shadowy foliage that her transparent nakedness loveth, and where I caught her, who in flight is like a wind-blown petal, caught her and caressed with her, defying her warning, so did it befall. For as she charmed me, so she bewitched me and forgave me in love — ... (498/VI 660)

To the initiated reader, however, this enigmatic confession makes complete sense. Even the veiled "O homo fuge" motif in its second variation, Adrian's musical setting of Eichendorff's poem *Zwielicht*, is implicitly present in the explicit warning of "twilight" or "twilit" dangers to which the composer so willingly fell prey.

Adrian never performs his last composition for the hand-picked audience, since he collapses after the first dissonant chord. But in describing the work for the reader, Serenus, in another of his self-adulatory observations, detects the recurrence of the five-note, musico-verbal cipher with which Adrian's expedition into modern music had been inaugurated. Exhibiting his usual pedantic zeal, Serenus recapitulates for the reader more remote events, making certain that no key concepts are omitted:

> Here I will remind the reader of a conversation I had with Adrian on a long-ago day, the day of his sister's wedding at Buchel, as we walked round the Cow Trough. He developed for me — under pressure of a headache — his idea of the "strict style," derived from the way in which, as in the lied *"O lieb Mädel, wie schlecht bist du,"* melody and harmony are determined by the permutation of a fundamental five-note motif, the symbolic letters h, e, a, e, e-flat. (486/VI 644-45)

To enumerate some of the central motifs reiterated at this point, one might single out: Cow Trough (Stable Hanne); wedding (the "marriage of music and words" in the *Lied* and the opera); headache (foreshadowing of death); *"O lieb Mädel, wie schlecht bist du!"* (Brentano's erotic escapades with wayward women; the same poet as pioneer of verbal musicality, much as Adrian has become the creator of a new tonal language); the *coincidentia oppositorum* or oxymoron aspect of all phenomena (by which the artist of the twentieth century simultaneously deploys and deplores a network of universal relationships); and finally, the five-note motif which, in its general contours and melodic intervals, resembles both the melodic yearning of the *Tristan* prelude and Isolde's love-death at the close of a music drama ostensibly rejected by Leverkühn for its bravado. Immediately prior to analyzing this facet of the *Lamentation*, Serenus noted that a close friend of the composer had recently introduced Adrian to a seventeenth-century work, a section of which "literally anticipates a passage in *Tristan*" (484/VI 642). Would it then fall totally outside of the realm of possibility that Wagner's motif of yearning and its coefficient, the love-death theme, might also have "anticipated a passage" in Leverkühn's oeuvre? The music of Hetæra, after all, does embody a very real erotic-thanatotic experience — albeit on a much less idealized, exalted, or "romanticized" plane.

Serenus contrasts the brief five-note motif from the past with the longer sequence of words and tones which supply the life's blood of the present *Weheklag*, only this time he adds a new twist:

> Long ago I said in these pages that in *Faustus* too that letter symbol, the Hetæra-Esmeralda figure, first perceived by me, very often governs melody and harmony: that is to say, everywhere where there is a reference to the bond and the vow, the promise and the blood pact. (489/VI 648)

Adrian's pact was, indeed sealed in his blood, even though he later maintains in his farewell speech that the teleological predisposition to such an audacious step was latent in him. Long "before I dallied with the poison butterfly," he declares, "my froward soul in high mind and arrogance was on the way to Satan" (499/VI 661). The careful reader who has followed the course of the Melos-Eros-Thanatos configuration in its evolutionary, if not revolutionary, manifestations is aware that what Adrian glosses over in silence or, at best circumscribes only obliquely, has been carefully and fully "orchestrated" by larger-than-life forces. These, however, were forces, with which this "hero" (like all those "with a thousand faces" traced by Joseph Campbell),[16] had to come to terms — only on his own terms.

C.   The Paradigmatic and Enigmatic Frau von Tolna

It was noted at the outset of this chapter that the terms "major" and "minor" in the context of *Doctor Faustus* should be viewed from a twofold perspective. Hetæra Esmeralda plays a major role in Adrian's career and creative life, even though the duration of her actual appearance is minimal and the mode of eroticism she represents (and which is embodied in her musical signature) would most likely be set in a minor key. Frau von Tolna's function in the

---

[16]The reference, of course, is to Campbell's *The Hero with a Thousand Faces* (Princeton: Princeton University Press, 1968).

overall scheme of the novel is minor, even though the influence she exerts on Adrian's life and work is set in a distinctly "major" tonality. Some astute, early detective work by a Thomas Mann scholar has led to the hypothesis — still in vogue after almost forty years — that the two women can be considered identical, if one weighs carefully all the factual data and fictional inferences supplied by the author.[17] The cleverly adduced prima faciæ evidence marshaled to undergird the Tolna-Esmeralda connection includes a variety of factors: common Hungarian backgrounds; an entomological pun based on two related concepts (Ægeridæ — a clear-wing moth; Egeria — a woman advisor or companion — but as a proper noun for a "nymph," it forms the root stem of Ægeridæ); etymological-phonological links (the German word for "emerald," *Smaragd*, and its Spanish equivalent, *esmeralda*); and a hidden acrostic (the quotation of a line of Greek verse which roughly equates in its letter constellation with the word "hetaira," an alternate spelling of "hetæra").[18]

The two women embody polar forms of love which might be broadly termed Eros and Caritas respectively, but it is also only in the relative distribution of these components of human passion and humane compassion that they differ and, in a sense, complement each other. Frau von Tolna, for instance, eschews all personal contact with Adrian, yet she pursues her "prey" with the same relentless determination with which Leverkühn hunted down Hetæra. Rather than use images from the hunt for Frau von Tolna, however, it might be more appropriate to couch her dogged devotion to the apostate Leverkühn in terms of a religious apostle. Much as a devout follower of a faith would visit holy shrines, so she makes pilgrimages to every place where the composer had lived, moved, and had his being — literally from the cradle to the grave. She supports his work financially, much as the individual of firm religious conviction tithes, and she does not fail to pay her last respects to Adrian — albeit incognita — as his body is lowered to its final resting place in 1940. Hetæra was intimately associated with a single major composition by Adrian (the Brentano Songs), even though her thematic signature "whispers magically ... throughout his work" (155/VI 207). In a similar manner, Frau von

---

[17]Oswald, "The Enigma of Frau von Tolna," 250-51.

[18]For more recent findings concerning Frau von Tolna (which, however, do not refute Oswald but rather simply introduce additional information), see *Thomas Mann und Ungarn*, ed. Antal Mádl and Judit Györi (Vienna: Böhlau, 1977), 53-60.

Tolna is primarily allied with one composition in the avant-garde idiom, the *Apocalypsis cum figuris*, a religiously tinged oratorio based on Albrecht Dürer's series of woodcuts and certain apocryphal texts. And yet the principle which she represents, that of aid and assistance through unseen forces "from above," likewise serves as a dominant theme in Leverkühn's major works of the 1906-1930 period.

The Hungarian noblewoman "that fine and scrupulous love" (390/VI 517), as a force of higher inspiration from a "sphere of love and faith, in a word the eternal feminine" (390/VI 517), was first drawn to Adrian's attention by the journalist Desiderius Fehér. The latter is an intermediary, whose rather commonplace Hungarian patronymic and Latin, humanistically tinged forename suggestive of emotional fervor, are symbolically well suited for the mediating role he plays. Anonymity (the nondescript name Fehér and von Tolna's carefully concealed identity) and sublimated personal desire are in such instances paramount. Desiderius speaks of the "high intellectual level and religious content of the music; its pride and despair, its diabolic cleverness, amounting to afflatus" (390/VI 517). Indeed, Fehér did not discover Adrian's compositions by himself. Instead he was alerted to them by "the shrewdest and most initiate connoisseur" of this music, Adrian's warmest admirer, a "woman of the world" who, however, had restrained her own desires by the "ascetic renunciation of any direct approach" (391/VI 519).[19]

The behind-the scenes patroness, Frau von Tolna, although not in the best of health and suffering from serious skin disorder (shades of Hetæra?) proved to be a world-traveler of boundless energy. We learn that she had attended, in the fashion of a "devout pilgrim" (392/VI 520), every performance of Adrian's music. The fact that she had not even omitted Italy from her itinerary gives rise to the conjecture of whether she might be identified with the

---

[19]The parallelism of Adrian's relationship to Frau von Tolna and that of Tschaikowsky to Frau von Meck is alluded to by Mann himself in his long exegesis of the novel, Die Entstehung des Doktor Faustus (Frankfurt am Main: Bermann-Fischer, 1949), 34. See also in this regard the remarks of the author to his musical mentor, Theodor Adorno (Dichter über ihre Dichtungen III, 61): "Thus I used, in the fashion of a montage, the motif of the invisible admirer and beloved, Tschaikowsky's Mrs. Meck, whom he never met and whom he avoided in personal contact." Hanspeter Brode, however, in his analysis of the "Thomas-Mann-Literatur 1974-1976," *Deutsche Vierteljahrsschrift für Literaturwissenschaft und Geistesgeschichte,* 50 (1976): 596-618, underscores the author's deliberate "strategies of deception" and his "game of hide-and-seek" with the reader, especially with reference to this novel (615). Therefore, we are admonished to take such bland statements of "fact" cum grano salis, even in nonfictional contexts.

mysterious Mme. de Coniar, "a lady of indefinite origins who patronized art and artists" (219/VI 292). De Coniar's plush villa, teeming with a host of international celebrities — including several Hungarians — was also frequented by Adrian. Of course, this potential *de Coniar-von Tolna* association would only be valid if Adrian never actually saw his Italian hostess; the novel, however, leaves this in limbo by not saying whether he did or not.

At a loss as to what designation to apply to Frau von Tolna, this enigmatic figure in Adrian's life (a "protecting deity, an Egeria, a soul-mate?" [392/VI 521]),[20] discreetly evades the issue of nomenclature by merely recording what she did for the composer. For instance, she sent him a jeweled Renaissance ring inset with a pure, pale green emerald, which once must have belonged to a Christian churchman, but which is inscribed with a pagan-Greek couplet concluding with the caveat: "Flee, profane one! [sic] Depart!" (393/VI 521). This inscription constitutes the last in the series of admonitions in Adrian's life, each of which was ambiguous in its message and none of which had been heeded by him. These included Eichendorff's poem "*Zwielicht*", the Latin command *O homo fuge!*, and Hetæra's fivefold warning to Adrian. But in addition to containing this final, obscure inscription, the ring also has carved on its surface the vignette of a winged, snakelike monster "whose tongue was clearly arrow-shaped" (393/VI 521). The arrow image brings to mind not only earlier references to Amor's weapon, but it also recalls the concept of Adrian as a man struck by the "arrow of fate" (153/VI 203) setting out from Leipzig in pursuit of the brown wench. Finally, there are also overtones of the diabolic adversary's quotation from a Brentano poem about a poisoned draught and "the wound the serpent/ Fastened and firmly sucked" (228/VI 305) when referring to Hetæra.

It is not without significance that Adrian wears the emerald ring from Frau von Tolna on his left hand — warning inscription and carved serpent notwithstanding — while working on the *Apocalypsis cum figuris* in an almost ritual fashion. The title of the oratorio pays homage to Dürer's series of woodcuts, but the inspiration comes from an eclectic mélange of prophetically apocalyptic sources. The piece was conceived by Leverkühn in 1919, only after a protracted period of severe head pain had subsided and the even greater

---

[20]Oskar Seiffert, *A Dictionary of Classical Antiquities*, rev. and ed. Henry Nettleship and J.E. Sandys (Cleveland: World Publishing, 1961), 207, notes that an Egeria was the mythical companion and advisor to the legendary rulers of Rome. Oswald, in "The Enigma," 251, notes that the Daughters of Egeria, The Ægeriadæ, are, entomologically speaking, also a class of clear-winged moths.

suffering of mankind in general, World War I, had come to a catastrophic end. Most of the texts which served to augment Dürer's pictorial representations were supplied by Frau von Tolna during a period when, as we learn somewhat abruptly and anticlimactically, she and Adrian corresponded with one another. Frau von Tolna is also credited with having given the composer helpful hints with regard to the structure of the work, and she arranges for both its publication and also for the review of it by Fehér in the journal *Anbruch*.

One of the central episodes in this choral work with orchestral accompaniment focuses on the "great whore, the woman on the beast" (357/VI 475), a figure stemming from the lamentations of the prophet Ezekiel, but which, nevertheless, bears a resemblance to Dürer's "portrait study ... of a Venetian courtesan" (357/VI 475). The idea of a musical work built around an exotic courtesan or concubine ("hetæra") certainly had its precedent in Leverkühn's oeuvre; but there is in this instance no specific tonal signature or melodic phrase as had previously been the case with Hetæra Esmeralda. Anonymity had been and remains the hallmark of Frau von Tolna's association with Adrian and his music.

Along with the less than exalted eroticism in the *Apocalypsis* there is in this work a death component far removed from any grandiose, romantically tinged love-death or death-in-love proportions. From the *Apocrypha* and from Dante's *Divine Comedy* come visions of terror. We observe landscapes "swarming with bodies ..." where "Charon's bark unloads its freight" and "the damned man, voluptuous in flesh, ... makes horrid descent" while "angels perform staccato on trumpets of destruction" (358/VI 476). The juxtaposition of images from Christianity's New Testament book of Revelation and pagan Greek mythology (even via Dante) with the trumpets of the Last Judgment accompanying Charon's bark on the river Styx, is striking. Such interplay constitutes another variation of that kind of *coincidentia oppositorum* which has become integral to Adrian's musical handiwork. This is graphically illustrated by the musical settings themselves, the very life's blood of which, as Serenus' subsequent analysis reveals, is the evolutionary coexistence of the most blatant contraries and aesthetic oxymora. For example, "speaking" choruses are transformed into "the richest vocal music"; "sounds which begin as mere noise, ... savage, fanatical, ritual, ... end by arriving at the purest music;" the work strives to reveal "in the language of music ... the beast in man as well as his sublimest stirrings" (373-74/VI 496).

Consequently, what is morally most reprehensible on the human plane can be transfigured musically into incomprehensibly beautiful sound: "the part of the 'Whore of Babylon, the Woman on the Beast, with whom the kings of the earth have committed fornication,' is, surprisingly enough a most graceful coloratura of great virtuosity; its brilliant runs blend at times with the orchestra exactly like a flute" (375/VI 498). The interchange between voices and orchestra, by which "the chorus is 'instrumentalized,' the orchestra as it were 'vocalized' " (375/VI 498), thereby obliterating lines of demarcation, is something which disturbs Serenus. The humanist in him likes clear-cut distinctions and well-established boundaries. But this does not prevent him from becoming a most articulate spokesman for this aesthetic-ethical coincidence of opposites: "precisely here, is revealed to me, in a way to make my heart stop beating, the profoundest mystery of this music, which is a mystery of identity" (378/VI 502).

The "strict style" had long ago been inaugurated with "dear-evil" Hetæra Esmeralda, the whore of Leipzig, and her signature motif in the Brentano songs on a relatively small scale. The dichotomous unity of her being had supplied a foretaste of what Serenus subsequently characterizes as the essential feature of the apocalyptic oratorio: "the substantial identity of this most blest with the most accurst, the inner unity of the chorus of child angels and the hellish laughter of the damned" (486/VI 645). And exactly how does this mystery of identity or "inner unity" relate to the strict style of musical composition? Serenus tries to supply an answer with reference to Adrian's compositional skill "in making the unlike the like" (378/VI 502). The upshot of the procedure is the attainment of ultimate co-incidence and coexistence:

> passages of horror just before heard are given, indeed, to the indescribable children's chorus at quite a different pitch, and in changed orchestration and rhythms; but in the searing, susurrant tones of spheres and angels there is not one note which does not occur, with rigid correspondence, in the hellish laughter. (378-79/VI 502-503)

So it would appear that the music instigated by the eroticism of the "infernal female" in Hetæra Esmeralda and that inspired by the caritative "eternal feminine" represented by the altruistic love of Frau von Tolna might stand in a similar relationship of identity. Leverkühn had devised a form of composition which could undergird the conjecture of a secret coalescence of prostitute and patroness. Direct sexual relations and an indirect, but sexless, relationship (abstinence from any physical involvement) lead to a musical work whose quintessential feature rests upon the same kind of paradoxical identity of contraries reflected in the nature of the respective women themselves. "Eva" (the syndrome of original sin through seduction) and "Ave" (the promise of mediation and ultimate redemption), Esmeralda's name ("emerald") and von Tolna's emerald ring may have a lot more in common than the etymological affinities which bind them would suggest.

Frau von Tolna offers Adrian a standing invitation to visit her palatial estate in Hungary. The composer finally does travel there with the violinist Rudi Schwerdtfeger following the latter's concert in Vienna. But the outcome of this Hungarian escapade is a far cry from his previous adventure with Hetæra in the Hungarian city of Pressburg. Leverkühn, suffering from one of his now more frequent and severe sieges of headache (395/VI 524), does not engage in a heterosexual affair with his benefactress (who remains behind in Vienna after the performance, where she had just been another anonymous face in the crowd). Instead he indulges in a homosexual tryst with the instrumental virtuoso.

Frau von Tolna, even if severed from any actual ties of identity with the Leipzig prostitute, can be said to have loved Adrian from afar, exemplifying a mode of altruistic *caritas*. This stands in contrast to the dominance of eros and its physiological consequences in the case of Hetæra. Yet the link of both women to the thanatotic, although antithetical, is nevertheless noteworthy. In contrast to Hetæra, who, in spite of her attempts to warn Adrian of her body, functions ultimately as the direct agent of death, Frau von Tolna's role in the terminal stages of Leverkühn's life is much more ethereal. It is shrouded in the same cloak of unresolved mystery and speculation that surround her long-standing religious devotion to, and dealings with, the composer. Assuming that Frau von Tolna is actually the unidentified graveside figure at Leverkühn's burial site, "a stranger, a veiled unknown, who disappeared as the first clods fell on the coffin" (510/VI 676), then it is evident that this woman departs from Adrian's world as mysteriously as she had entered it. She functions as an enigmatic "minor" figure to be sure, but one who is paradigmatic in her role as the eternal feminine that inspired from afar and above, careful to preserve her anonymity, and yet not without a major impact and influence on the man and his music. Conversely, Hetæra Esmeralda, the embodiment of the erotic in a "minor" mode, likewise plays a major role in Adrian's career and creativity as the "infernal female," an ambience which, in the short run brings aesthetic inspiration to the artist both thematically and structurally, but, concomitant with this, growing physical deterioration and, in the long run, death. Finally, if one ascribes to the hypothesis of an Hetæra-von Tolna identity,[21] then one might observe that the prostitute, who was explicitly manifest in Adrian's most innovative music by her signature motiv, is implicitly present at the graveside of the composer as the catalytic force which claimed his life. The anonymous patroness, on the other hand, is manifestly absent as any explicit motif or theme in Leverkühn's works, but is explicitly in attendance at the moment when the grave claims him. This speculation, of course, is contingent upon another conjecture: that the unidentified, "veiled woman" is, indeed, Frau von Tolna (the ultimate stage of that anonymity, which seemed well suited to every phase of her relationship with Adrian Leverkühn).

---

[21]The hypothesis of a concealed identity of Hetæra and Tolna is supported, even though only obliquely, by a parallel phenomenon, the "secret identity" of Zeitblom and Leverkühn, which Mann himself revealed in his *Entstehung des Doktor Faustus* when he alluded to these two "protagonists, who had too much to conceal, namely the secret of their identity" (XI 204). This topic together with a host of other hidden identities in the novel are analyzed at considerable length and in convincing detail by Eckhard Heftrich in *Über Thomas Mann,* 173-325.

4   "The Unanswered Question"

HAVING EXAMINED TWO PRINCIPAL statements of the Melos-Eros-Thanatos complex in the preceding chapter, it almost seems anti-climactic to trace further manifestations of the constellation throughout the remainder of the novel. And yet, such a procedure can help reinforce the "through-composed" nature of Mann's prose and reveal that meticulous degree of artistic exponentiation which continuously and conscientiously monitors the overall design. The result is that even the smallest details undergird the main thrust of the work, without blurring, in the process, the total picture by any too brilliant display in the subsidiary parts. After all, "Relationship is everything" is not only a credo of Adrian Leverkühn, but also a credential of his creator.

The closing chapter is divided into three sub-sections: 1) *A Devilishly Diabolic Debate* presents a detailed overview of the Melos-Eros-Thanatos elements in the central mono- or dialogue which Adrian records during his Italian journey; 2) *Human Relations* investigates the music, love and death configuration with respect to subsidiary figures in the work; 3) *Musical Correlations* focuses on the matter in which Leverkühn incorporates elements of these personal relationships into his innovative compositions.

A.   A Devilishly Diabolic Debate[1]

Falling somewhere between his Pyrrhic conquest of Hetæra and his vicarious encounter with Frau von Tolna comes Adrian's confrontation with his alter ego in the form of an adversarial apparition in Italy. The analysis of this conversation — real, imagined, or whatever — will be divided into several phases, corresponding to the metamorphoses undergone by the antagonist or the "other self." The respective topics of the discussion can be coordinated with the tripartite subject of this investigation, only here in the altered sequence: Eros, Melos and Thanatos.

The fact that the entire scene was recorded by Adrian on music note paper is, according to Serenus, a sheer accident. But this constitutes another of the narrator's misconceptions, akin to his assumption that Leverkühn's musical allusions before and after his bordello episode were merely a diversionary

---

[1]*Webster's Third New International Dictionary of the English Language,* ed. Philip Babcock Gove (Springfield, Mass.: G & C. Merriam, 1964), 618-19, under the word "devil" traces the related adjectival form "diabolic" back to the Greek 'diaballein' meaning to throw across" ('dia' signifying "through" and 'ballein' "throw"), in the sense of causing disruption, chaos and confusion by intervening, interrupting, etc.

cover-up. They were actually a dis-covery or un-covering of the links between the erotic and music, the musical erotic. What Serenus regards as incidental or accidental (the use of music paper) is really integral and essential. Once again, the narrator fails to see the forest (the interdependence of love, music, and death) for the sake of the individual trees (the independence of Melos, Eros, and Thanatos). Therefore, here as elsewhere, it is sometimes incumbent upon the critic to read against the grain of the fictional narrator's interpretation.

The background for the familiar configuration is established by the fact that Adrian reads Kierkegaard's *Don Giovanni* essay on the musical erotic after having suffered the entire day from headaches. "I had lien in the dark with irksome mygrym, retching and spewing, as happeth with the severer seizures" (222/VI 297). At this point, the adversarial dialogue-partner appears amid a wave of coldness in the first of the three manifestations or "masks" which he dons during the protracted conversations. In this initial, most diabolic appearance, he emphasizes primarily the erotic component and its function in their pact through a sequence of passing references: to Adrian's score for the incipient opera *Love's Labour's Lost* (225/VI 299); to the leaf butterfly; to Adrian's "pretty song with the letter symbol" (228/VI 304); and, by devious circumlocution, to the venereal infection (the English translation "when you ... summoned your French beloved to you" is an inadequate rendering of the German "als du ... dir ... die lieben Franzosen holtest" [229/VI 305]). With a touch of satanic thoroughness, he does not fail to draw attention to Andersen's Little Sea-Maid and her bargain. The inference seems to be that she would make an ideal "sweetheart" for the composer because of the ties between the sharp, knife-like pains she suffered for her infractions and Adrian's agonizing "mygryms" endured for his (230/VI 308).[2] Finally, and most devastatingly, the speaker enumerates in scientific jargon the insidious manner in which the spirochæta pallida bacterium, "our pale Venus" (231/VI 309), is even now advancing on its stealthy, osmotic path to the cerebrum: "the meta-spirochætose, that is the meningeal process ... the little ones had a passion for

---

[2]The figure of the little sea-maid from Hans Christian Andersen's fairy tale has aroused only peripheral critical attention, as for instance Barbara Fass, "The Little Mermaid and the Artist's Quest for a Soul," *Comparative Literature Studies* 9 (1972): 290-302. Toward the close of the novel Leverkühn refers to her by the name Hyphialta. In *Dichtungen über ihre Dichtungen,* III, 130, Mann notes: "The name Hyphialta I took from daemonic literature. I noted: 'Incubi or Succubae, Ephialtæ, feminine or masculine devils, who unite with men or women, [this being] the general view of the venerable Church patriarchs and teachers.'" For a plausible explanation of the introduction of the name Hyphialta into the text, see Alfred Hoelzel, "Leverkühn, the Mermaid, and Echo: A Tale of Faustian Incest," *Symposium* 42 (1988): 3-16.

the upper storey, a special preference for the head region, the meninges, the dura mater, the tentorium, and the pia ..." (233/VI 311). It is at this point that this "friend and cohabitant of Esmeralda" reveals with malicious pleasure, that Spengler, although an infected Esmeraldus, will never experience "a metastasis into the metaphysical, metavenereal, metainfectivus ..." (232/VI 310). His lot is to languish in the limbo of mediocrity.

Adrian, for his part, proves to be no slouch in parrying some of these thrusts. By dubbing his opponent "Black Kaspar" or Samiel, he tries to neutralize this foe in terms of chordal progressions from Wolf's Glen scene of *Der Freischütz*. It was from this romantic opera par excellence, that he had played excerpts on the piano in the brothel as a defense mechanism against the physical allure of the prostitutes. But the relentless foe taunts him that his weapon this time is verbal rather than musical: "Where then is your C-minor fortissimo of stringed tremoli, wood and trombones, ingenious bug to fright children, the romantic public, coming out of the F-sharp minor of the Glen as you out of your abyss — I wonder I hear it not!" (227/VI 303).[3]

The great debater concludes his initial onslaught by underscoring Eros' dire consequence for the artist with a predisposition such as that of Leverkühn; his demise was "in his blood" before it actually entered into his blood:

> The mygrim, the point of attack for the knife-pains of the little sea-maid — after all, you have them from him [Adrian's father].... Moreover, I have spoken quite correctly: osmosis, fluid diffusion, the proliferation process.... . You have there the spinal sac with the pulsating column of fluid therein, reaching to the cerebrum, to the meninges, in whose tissues the furtive veneral meningitis is at its soundless stealthy work. But our little ones could not reach into the inside, into the parenchyma, however much they are drawn, ... without fluid diffusion, osmosis....
> (235/VI 313)

After his first metamorphosis, the opponent now a bespectacled intellectual, moves to the musical dilemmas confronting any twentieth-century composer worth his salt. By extension, this quandary confronts all truly creative

---

[3] Both Kaspar and Samiel, the Black Hunter, are figures from Weber's *Der Freischütz* and each has satanic ties and dealings in the occult arts. Speaking of this opera, Mann notes (Dichter über ihre Dichtungen, III, 106): "Kaspar is the villain of the piece, in conspiracy with the devil.... Samiel is the name of the devil. Since, however, in old legends concerning the devil, the evil one is designated as black Käsperlin, the identity of Kaspar and Samiel thus becomes apparent."

spirits in the modern era, whether they be poet, painters, writers, musicians, or whatever. In cataloguing the formidable canon of the forbidden imposed by traditional music over the centuries and today only suitable for parody, he outlines the arsenal of difficulties to be surmounted in the course of the "pilgrimage on peas" to which artistic creativity has been reduced (238/VI 318). His credentials for undertaking this task seem impeccable, based on the kind of mental gymnastics he performs and the clever *coincidentia oppositorum* arguments he marshals to drive home his points: "The Devil ought to know something about music," he maintains, citing Kierkegaard's treatise on *Don Giovanni* and the musical erotic. That Christian author "knew and understood my particular relation to this beautiful art — the most Christian of all arts, he finds — but Christian in reverse, as it were: introduced and developed by Christianity indeed, but then rejected and banned as the Divel's Kingdom.... A highly theological business, music — the way sin is" (242/VI 322-23). Kierkegaard had a true passion for music, but then "there is true passion only in the ambiguous and ironic" (242/VI 323). The adversary's radical remedy for a "breakthrough" from the present stalemate, the cure leading from the "paralyzing difficulties of the time" (243/VI 324) to the production of new music is, paradoxically, sickness; "that creative, genius-giving disease, disease that rides on high horse over all hindrances, and springs with drunken daring from peak to peak.... morbid genius, made genius by disease" (242/VI 323-24).

Following his second metamorphosis, the protean opponent, now in the guise of one of Adrian's lecturers at the University of Halle, calls upon all the devices of rhetoric and sophistry at his disposal to both answer and avoid answering the composer's probing question. What will be the "payment in pains to be made now and again for the higher life"? (244/VI 325). What is the ultimate price for the euphoric powers of creativity that "outweigh the pangs of the little sea-maid"? (243/VI 324). In response to Adrian's specific query concerning the torment to be endured after death, there comes an evasive response couched in terms of the inexpressibility topos. This is followed by the lame excuse that in trying to describe the indescribable, one must be content with symbolism rather than contend with direct statement. When these explanations fail to satisfy Leverkühns's curiosity, the *advocatus diaboli* finally lays his cards on the table by arguing the reciprocity of sin and salvation — another *coincidentia oppositorum* which Adrian then paraphrases in his own terms: "A capacity for sin so healless that it makes its man despair from his heart of redemption — that is the true theological way to salvation" (247/VI 329).

This formulation, at almost the precise midpoint of the novel, gives renewed impetus to the "dear-evil" girl oxymoron at the heart of the already completed thirteen Brentano songs and serves as the guiding principle for the major compositions later. This is especially true for the interdependence of heaven and hell, for the reciprocity of harmony and dissonance in the *Apocalypsis cum figuris* and, above all, for the cool, intellectual calculation and emotional fervor in Leverkühn's culminating work, *Dr. Fausti Weheklag.*

Resuming his original appearance after the two intervening metamorphoses, the clever foe likewise returns to his opening theme for a final reprise. Again we hear of the intimate links of the erotic with the thanatotic. The risks Adrian took by forsaking "the Good Boke" for "the figures, characters, and incantations of music" (248/VI 330) will pave the way for a personal "apocalypse with figures." Embracing music is correlated with Hetæra's embrace, together with all its concomitant pleasures and pains: "Thus it was our busily prepensed plan that you should run into our arms, that is, of my little one, Esmeralda, and that you got it, the illumination, the aphrodisiacum of the brain ..." (248/VI 331). The strategies of the adversary in this summation are not too different from the stratagems of the traditional composer in designing a piece of music in the sonata form (A-B-A^1) or Exposition — Development — Recapitulation. There is even a return to the "tonic" key in the concluding section in the sense that the speaker resumes his original appearance and restates his premises in terms of the fundamental set of themes.

But when the diabolic opponent adds the coda or codicil that any modality of love, from unadulterated lust to altruistic adoration, from base carnality to "sweet" charity, is henceforth prohibited to Adrian, the latter detects a glaring contradiction. The glib antagonist has hoisted himself by his own petard, so to speak, since a form of Eros was the basis for their bargain to begin with: "What I have invited, and wherefore you allege that I have promised you — what is then the source of it, prithee, but love, even if that poisoned by you with God's sanction? The bond in which you assert we stand has itself to do with love, you doating fool" (248/VI 332). Sensing, then, that he has indeed gotten himself into a "circulus vitiosus" (or better yet in this case, "diabolicus," derived from the German *Teufelskreis*), the adversary seeks to escape by playfully qualifying his previous blanket injunction against love:

Do, re, mi! ... Love is forbidden you, in so far as it warms. Thy life shall be cold, therefore thou shalt love no human being.... A general chilling of your life and your relations to men lies in the nature of things — rather it lies already in your nature; in feith we lay upon you nothing new, the little ones make nothing new and strange out of you, they only ingeniously strengthen and exaggerate all that you already are. The coldness in you is perhaps not prefigured, as well as the paternal head paynes out of which the pangs of the little sea-maid are to come? (249/VI 332)

The creator of music must be humanly frigid in order to fan the torrid fires of aesthetic productivity: "Cold we want you to be, that the fires of creation shall be hot enough to warm yourself in" (249/VI 332). The art of love will, in the case of this composer, be restricted to the love of art. Yet heat and cold, as has been the case with so many of the polar opposites encountered thus far, are to stand in a mutually reciprocal, "sympathetic" or symbiotic relationship, rather than in one of antithesis or antagonism. The culmination of the warmth-coldness dialectic comes to the fore in Adrian's last composition which draws its very life's blood from the paradox of a coolly calculated fervor, or as Serenus, with his customary picayune pedantry, summarizes:

> the recovery, I would not say the reconstruction — and yet for the sake of exactness I will say it — of expressivism, of the highest and profoundest claim of feeling to a stage of intellec-tuality and formal strictness, which must be arrived at in order that we may experience a reversal of this calculated coldness and its conversion into a voice expressive of the soul and a warmth and sincerity of creature confidence. (485/VI 643)

Of course, any comments of Serenus must be weighed on the scales of skepticism since he is, admittedly, a biased narrator not always equal to the task he has selected to — or been selected to — perform. For instance, his closing comment on the dialogue between Adrian and the latter's adversary (or psychological alter ego) deserves careful scrutiny. Serenus maintains that his transcription of the great debate bore all the earmarks of his "rueful loyalty," even while admitting that he transferred the text from "music-paper to my [Serenus'] manuscript" (251/VI 334). In his ingenuousness — which he sometimes mistakes for ingeniousness — Serenus fails to recognize that the elimination of the musical staves may contribute to a tidier report, but, in the long run, it deprives this central confrontation of an essential dimension of symbolic significance: that Melos stood squarely in the background of the verbal dual, even when Eros and Thanatos ostensibly dominated the foreground.

B.   Human Relations: Music and the Munich Social Scene

Adrian's liaison with Hetæra Esmeralda (1905-1906) remains a clandestine affair, until, in the dénouement of the novel, he reveals her identity obliquely in a confession to a farewell gathering of friends and acquaintances at

Pfeiffering (1930). The role of Frau von Tolna, by its very nature, had been — and had to remain — *sub rosa*. Therefore one might say that the world at large was unaware of the dramatic force — positive as well as negative — which these modes of erotic bonding played in Adrian's career and creativity. This situation changed gradually once Leverkühn left rustic Buchel, medieval Kaisersaschern, and the quaint university town of Halle, and then radically after his Leipzig-Pressburg experience. In spite of his lingering proclivity for solitude at Pfeiffering in Bavaria, Adrian frequented the Munich salon of the Rodde family and attended the soirées held at the homes of leading industrialists such as Schlaginhaufen's or Bullinger's. In each new environment there was a musical-erotic-thanatotic ambience of varying intensity and importance.

Not all the salon devotees need — or deserve — consideration in the framework of this investigation, especially when they are amateur performers of inferior status or even generous hosts of major celebrities from the musical world. Yet the appearance of professional artists such as the corpulent soprano Tania Orlanda is a noteworthy event, not only because of her renditions of two excerpts from Wagner's *Tristan und Isolde* with Adrian as her accompanist, but also due to the specific musical selections chosen. Leverkühn, ostensibly the reluctant Wagnerite who had once spoken derogatorily of the "voluptuosity" of this music drama and its "bull-fight character of a theatrical mysticism robust in its corruption" nevertheless acquiesces to perform these "*Tristan* orgies" in public. Isolde's "Frau Minne kennst du noch?" obviously stresses the element of adulterous Eros beyond the bounds of medieval convention, while the ecstatic tones of "Die Fackel, und wär's meines Lebens Licht, lachend sie zu löschen zagt' ich nicht" clearly embodies the Thanatos component. Serenus, also no friend of "Wagner's work, loud and violent as it was" (277/VI 369), was nevertheless almost brought to tears by this performance. Adrian, however, as befits a composer coolly aware of his compatriot's calculated musical tricks to arouse emotions to the maximum level of sensuality, simply "smiled when he rose from the piano-stool" (278/VI 369).

The eroticism of Tania's *Tristan* excerpts can still be relegated to the lofty realm of a romantic love-in-death, only ironically relativized by Adrian's knowing smile on the verge of Serenus' tears. The other aspect of love from a higher domain, "caritas" as a mode of divine concern or disembodied human affection, dominates in the case of several other women who, like Frau von Tolna, find an almost religious calling in tending the needs of the composer. In the orbit of the Munich salon there appears a cluster of such women. These include the ubiquitous Jeanette Scheurl, a physically unattractive lady and quixotic writer (with a real life prototype) who is also a talented pianist and musicologist of sorts.[4] Like Adrian's two female attendants at Pfeiffering, Meta Nackedey, a one-time piano teacher (312/VI 416) who holds Leverkühn's works sacred (313/VI 417) and Kunigunde Rosenstiel "as almost all Jews ... , very musical" (313-14/VI 417), Jeanette Scheurl lovingly serves the composer and the cause of modern music with self-sacrificing — almost self-effacing — devotion. Jeanette, "whose society was always a comfort to him" (411/VI 545), also proves to be a serene muse for Adrian's distraught soul late in his life, when she plays Mozart for him on the square grand piano at the Schweigestill farm in Pfeiffering.

Jeanette Scheurl functions as the silently suffering witness to Adrian Leverkühn's last loves (in defiance of the diabolic prohibition) which are: heterosexual, bi- or homosexual, and a-sexual in nature. At a dinner gathering in Zurich, for instance, Jeanette's place at the table is taken by the fetching, young Marie Godeau with whom Adrian becomes infatuated and later woos in vain by proxy. Jeanette accompanies another of Leverkühn's ardent admirers, the violinist Rudi Schwerdtfeger (who, by both destiny and design, serves as Adrian's unsuccessful proxy wooer) on the piano. Finally, following the agonizing death of the beloved, divine child, Adrian's nephew Nepomuk Schneidewein, when the composer reaches his spiritual nadir, Jeanette is, as ever, at his side supplying him with music from the seventeenth century to console his faltering spirits.

In spite of her own dire financial straits, Jeanette undertakes the journey to Frankfurt for the premiere of the *Apocalypsis cum figuris* in 1926 (shades of Frau von Tolna's fetish for attending first performances). Upon her return the disciple dutifully reports to the master — a scene which Serenus captures with his usual engagingly equivocating style:

> Adrian especially prized this peasant-aristocrat, her presence had a beneficial and soothing effect on him, like a sort of guardian spirit. Actually I have seen him sitting hand in hand with her in a corner of the Abbot's room, silent and as it were in safe-keeping. This hand-in-hand was not like him, it was a change which I saw with emotion, even with pleasure, but yet not quite without anxiety. (453/VI 601)

---

[4]For some remarks concerning the role played by the quixotic Annette Kolb, Scheurl's real-life prototype, in Thomas Mann's career, see John Fetzer, "Faktisches und Fiktionales über Annette Kolb. Wechselbeziehungen zwischen ihrer Darstellung des Exillebens und der Darstellung ihres Lebens durch den exilierten Thomas Mann," in *Das Exilleben*, ed. Donald G. Daviau and Ludwig Fischer (Columbia, South Carolina: Camden House, 1982), 280-88.

At this time, in 1926, Adrian was in a very vulnerable state, having lost any creative spark, wallowing in intellectual stagnation, and hovering at the low-water mark of his health ("severe attacks of migraine confined him to darkness" [455/VI 603]). All this came in the wake of his shipwrecked marriage plans with Marie Godeau and the tragic loss of his intermediary in this venture, the violinist Rudi Schwerdtfeger, who also had been Adrian's own sexual partner during a brief affair in Hungary. Perhaps Serenus' anxiety at seeing Adrian "hand in hand" with Jeanette stems from the remote possibility of a "love on the rebound" relationship between Leverkühn and the intellectually challenging but "aristocratically ugly" woman "with a face like a sheep" (201/VI 269). This conjecture is reinforced somewhat by Serenus' later observation that it was Jeanette who brought the stymied Leverkühn, mired, with regard to his work, in a creative impasse, the chaconne of the seventeenth century composer, Jacopo Melani, "which literally anticipates a passage in *Tristan*" (484/VI 642).

If a hint of eroticism does surface in the Scheurl-Leverkühn relationship and find expression in her efforts to support his musical career, then the thanatotic component is also in evidence. For Jeanette, like the incognita Frau von Tolna, is one of the four guests (all women) at Adrian's graveside for the burial ceremony, after having helped nurse and nurture the fallen Icarus through his incoherent rantings and final collapse. But unlike the veiled stranger, who, perhaps in order to insure her anonymity, disappears as the first clods of earth clatter onto the coffin, Scheurl remains stoically at the grave site until the very end.

Adrian's most devastating musical, erotic, thanatotic experience stemming from the decadent world in Munich society is his sexual liaison with the concert violinist, Rudi Schwerdtfeger. This entails not only a homosexual encounter, but also a bizarre heterosexual love triangle in which the erstwhile male lovers now vie for the affections of the same woman (Marie Godeau). It concludes dramatically with a sensational shooting incident which claims the life of the virtuoso. And if this bi- or homosexual liaison were not awkward enough, Adrian chooses as his proxy wooer for the hand of Marie, none other than Rudi himself, fully aware that the latter is also in love with her. The violinist's surname, which in English would be rendered by something like "sword-maker," is reminiscent of the chivalric medieval knight and his heroic feats with this weapon. Rudi's "sword," of course, which is the "bow" he wields when performing in the concert hall, evokes at the same time phallic implications for the critics of the Freudian persuasion.[5]

[5]The literal meaning of Schwer(d)tfeger is, according to *The New Cassell's German Dictionary*, ed. Harold T. Betteridge (New York: Funk & Wagnalls, 1958), 420, "armourer, sword-cutler." However, one cannot overlook the phallic implications of the "sword" concept throughout

Since Serenus is particularly ill-disposed to Schwerdtfeger, the intimate of Adrian and the darling of the ladies, the impression the reader gains of the violinist through the narrator's jaundiced perspective is to be taken *cum grano salis*. It is certainly not tempered by the milk of human kindness. For example, in almost patronizing fashion, Serenus comments on the personal and professional life of the violinist, and maintains that he (Serenus) was deeply touched by the talented artist's premature death. At the very beginning of the novel, however, he had reported the demise of the "charming trifler and winner of hearts" (5-6/VI 13). Later he comments rather maliciously concerning Rudi's sexual proclivities: "He at once had his eye on Adrian, paid court to him, practically neglecting the ladies ..." (199/VI 266).

Immediately after the introduction of Rudi to the reader at the salon of the Rodde family, elements of the now familiar Melos-Eros-Thanatos triad loom on the horizon. The major trait of Rudi's personality, that of wooing and winning the favors of others, seems innocuous enough to Serenus until it takes on ominous overtones with regard to Leverkühn. There are periodical signs indicative of latent homosexuality in Rudi, such as his habit of taking Adrian by the arm. Inez Rodde's patent warning "You shouldn't give him the pleasure. He wants everything" (203/VI 272), is not heeded by the composer; this is another of his omissions which leads to the commission of what society might label an indiscretion.

Adrian insists on interpreting Schwerdtfeger's overtures strictly from the artistic standpoint: "What he wants ... is that I should write a violin concerto for him" (203/VI 272). This, of course, is also true. There are, consequently, dual aspects to the relationship of the soloist to the composer; non-procreative homosexuality and the symbiotically creative, a-sexual artistry (Rudi's desire for a violin concerto as a kind of "platonic child" [350/VI 467]). These two elements later fuse with the heterosexual (their mutual rivalry for the hand of Marie Godeau in marriage) in a wild mélange of Melos-Eros-Thanatos, as bizarre as was the roller-coaster life in Munich during the 1920s.

One final touch, to make the situation even more absurd. Rudi, as the wooer of Adrian's aesthetic and erotic favors, is not only commissioned by Leverkühn to woo Marie Godeau for him (Adrian) by proxy, but he (Rudi), in turn, although in love with Marie himself, is wooed by an unhappily married and sexually frustrated Inez Rodde-Institoris. Needless to say, Schwerdtfeger, because of his own vested interest, woos ineptly and unsuccessfully on behalf of Leverkühn. A cursory examination of this trio of wooers and the respective

literature, from the medieval heroic and courtly epics (*Das Nibelungenlied* and *Tristan und Isolde*) to more modern adaptions (*Der Ring des Nibelungen* of Wagner, in which Siegfried's sword is a central motif).

objects of their wooing will shed some new light on the Melos-Eros-Thanatos complex in its more aberrant manifestations.

Turning first to Rudi Schwerdtfeger and the "platonic child" he seeks from Adrian, the violinist presses for his concerto soon after becoming romantically involved (haplessly and hopelessly) with Inez Rodde-Institoris. This was, according to his confession to Serenus, against the grain of his own conscience and better judgment. Approaching Adrian on a day in 1919 when the latter is suffering from "severe head pains" (348/VI 463), Rudi whistles — perhaps in prophetically ironic fashion — the bourrée from the composer's opera *Love's Labour's Lost*, and confesses that he needs an original work by Leverkühn for his "purification" (350/VI 466). The latter is obviously a loaded term in view of the fact that Adrian's own confessional letter concerning his sexual transgression with Hetæra was dated "Purificationis."

Debunking his reputation as a shallow flirt and amoroso, Rudi denies having ever encouraged Inez romantically, claiming instead that the desperate passion was solely on her side: "I have never loved her, ... I always just had friendly and brotherly feelings for her ..." (349/VI 465). In performing his "knightly duty" (349/VI 465), however, he had become inextricably entangled in a web of love and intrigue from which he now needed to escape through the medium and mediation of a pure piece of music. The latter would constitute "the most symbolic expression for this need" (350/VI 466).

Rudi not only proposes the violin concerto in general terms, but also outlines specific compositional details, and his description reads like a combination of aggressive male impregnation and passive female conception:

And you would do it wonderfully, ... with an unheard-of simple and singable first theme in the main movement that comes in again after the cadenza.... But you don't need to do it like that, you don't need to have a cadenza at all, that is just a convention. You can throw them all overboard, even the arrangement of the movements, it doesn't need to have any movements, for my part you can have the allegro molto in the middle, a real "Devil's trill," and you can juggle with the rhythm, as only you can do, and the adagio can come at the end, as transfiguration — it couldn't be too unconventional. ... I want to get it into myself so I could play it in my sleep ... and love every note like a mother, and you would be the father — it would be between us like a child, a platonic child — yes, *our* concerto, that would be so exactly the fulfillment of everything that I understand by platonic. (350/VI 466-67)

Aside from the reproductive roles assigned to each partner in this act of aesthetic propagation which tosses aside all conventions of generic concern (concerto form) and gender considerations (the homosexual relationship being barren of offspring), such a proposal is intriguing from another standpoint: the Devil's trill midway in the work.[6] With regard to the overall format of *Doctor Faustus*, there is an equally "devilish" or diabolic passage at the core of this novel: the dialogue with the stranger in Italy. This is based both on structural symmetry (pages 225-250 of 510 in the English and pages 294-335 of 675 in the German) as well as thematic substance (the adversary's Satanic views on the interrelationship of music, love, and death in these particular pages).

Zeitblom, because of the prerogatives of the omniscient narrator (an outmoded stance which he, nevertheless, sometimes appropriates for himself) or simply due to his narratological ineptitude, clumsily discloses Rudi's "tragic end" (351/VI 467) at this juncture. He also compounds the felony, as it were, by appending a moralizing epithet (or epitaph) to the "sad success" of the entire ludicrous episode: "In the long run, the defenselessness of solitude against such a wooing was proved, certainly to the destruction of the wooer" (351/VI 467).

The popular, salon quality of the jointly conceived violin concerto is something on which Serenus dotes with spiteful glee, noting how this composition "falls somewhat out of the frame of Leverkühn's ruthlessly radical and uncompromising work as a whole" (409/VI 542). In other words, this artistic compromise definitely compromises Adrian's integrity and stature as an innovator and pioneer at the forefront of modern music. Serenus damns the composition with faint praise by labeling it "a kind of concession to concerto virtuosity" dedicated to Rudi personally (the German idiom "ihm [Rudi] ... auf den Leib geschrieben" [VI 542] can be considered a case of both unintentional and intentional verbal irony). This shallow type of showpiece enables the virtuoso to display all his instrumental pyrotechnics and it is more show than substance — as Serenus' prejudiced appraisal of the concerto reveals.

Even though the "hybrid production" (410/VI 544) bears no key signature, it is actually built on three distinct tonalities (B^b major, C-major, D-major), none of which, however, ever comes distinctly or dominantly to the forefront. This attribute perhaps serves as an objective correlative for the

---

[6]The allusion to the "devil's trill" refers, according to the *Musik-Lexikon* by H. J. Moser (Berlin: Max Hesse, 1935), 845, to a segment of the Violin Sonata by Giuseppe Tartini (1692-1770). In the section of this work entitled "reveries of the composer," Tartini dreams that the devil is sitting on his bed and performing a difficult trill with double stops. Great violin virtuosi such as Paganini were frequently linked to diabolical forces, since some felt such technical pyrotechnics could only stem from sources close to the devil.

dubious essence and sexual identity of the performer himself, since he proves to be both a "ladies' man" as well as a "man's man." The first movement in B^b major bears the telling superscript *andante amoroso* (409/VI 543), and the essence of its principal melody is, according to Serenus, "a dulcet tenderness bordering on mockery" (409/VI 543). This undoubtedly corresponds to that "unheard-of simple and singable first theme in the main movement" (350/VI 461) originally requested by Rudi. This lush theme incorporates notes from all three of the above tonalities, first as linear melody and then in the vertical harmony. Serenus must admit that this constitutes "a wonderful stroke of melodic invention, a rich, intoxicating cantilena of great breadth, which decidedly has something showy about it, and also a melancholy that does not lack in grace if the performer so interpret it" (410/VI 543). The qualifiers which Serenus intersperses throughout his interpretation ("concession," "hybrid," "showy," "if the performer ...") indicate that what he gives with one hand he takes away with the other. Acknowledgment of Adrian's skill and admiration for his inventiveness as a creator are paired with what Serenus perceives to be the shallowness of the rival who served as the inspiration and motivating force behind the creation.

Also in accord with Rudi's wishes is the reappearance of the captivating theme of "dulcet tones" (but not necessarily "bordering on mockery") in the third movement of the work as a set of variations. Concerning this, Serenus, with his usual parenthetically deprecating asides, makes the following observation:

The characteristically delightful thing about the invention is the unexpected and subtly accentuated rise of the melodic line after reaching a certain high climax, by a further step, from which then, treated in the most perfect, perhaps all too perfect taste, it flutes and sings itself away. It is one of those physically effective manifestations capturing head and shoulders, bordering on the "heavenly," of which only music and no other art is capable. And the tutti-glorification of just this theme in the last part of the variation movement brings the bursting out into the open C major. But just before it comes a bold flourish — a plain reminiscence of the first violin part leading to the finale of Beethoven's A-minor Quartet; only that here the magnificent phrase is followed by something different, a feast of melody in which the parody of being carried away becomes a passion which is seriously meant and therefore creates a somewhat embarrassing effect. (410/VI 543-44)

Several facets of this extensive description deserve commentary and clarification. First of all, the whole-tone progression of the principal theme in its upward thrust to C major is akin to (but by no means identical with) the modulation from B major to C major, that "brightening semitone step" in the hermit's prayer from the finale of *Der Freischütz*. This was the passage which Adrian struck on the piano when he entered the Leipzig bordello and to which reference had been made in his verbal parries with the adversary in Italy. In both instances the progression seems to suggest some form of redemption, of appeal to a higher echelon. Secondly, the allusion to Beethoven's A-minor Quartet also has precedents in the Hetæra Esmeralda world of the brothel. Adrian, upon his return from the Pressburg escapade, tries to persuade Serenus to attend a concert performance of this work with him. Zeitblom responds by spontaneously singling out the third movement of the quartet known as "Thanksgiving for Recovery." This is an ironic designation, since Leverkühn proves to be eminently unsuccessful in finding a physician who can help him recover from the malady he has contracted. Thirdly, one must consider Serenus' derogatory comment that Adrian's melodic festivity expresses, at best, an embarrassing parody of the genuine emotion in Beethoven's quartet, another slap in the face of the violin concerto. His previous assertion concerning the repetition of the thematic material from the first movement of the concerto in the finale, might be construed as a charge of creative impoverishment rather than a claim of inventiveness. Could this whole barrage of undercutting remarks be intended to convey the idea that Rudi's passion for Adrian is likewise merely a parody of genuine love? Does it imply that the homosexual act itself, at least in Serenus' eyes, is an empty imitation of the heterosexual relationship, since there is no hope of producing live offspring, but only a surrogate for real life in the form of the aesthetic artifact — and, in this case, a second-rate product at that?[7]

The basis for discussing the first and third movements of the concerto consecutively stems from the fact that both were constructed around a similar thematic substance. Some critics, of course, would maintain that this reflects a paucity of inspiration. Others might argue that metamorphoses of *idée fixe* material is a compositional strategy characteristic of several musical giants of the nineteenth century: Schumann, Berlioz, and Liszt, just to mention a few. The relegation of the second movement to the end of the analysis enables

---

[7]An interesting parallel to the "lifeless" offspring of the homosexual liaison is that found in Brentano's lyrics with regard to prostitutes; invariably these individuals are not meant to bear children or, if the whore does give birth, the infant is stillborn. See in this regard, Gabriele Brandstetter, *Erotik und Religiosität. Zur Lyrik Clemens Brentanos*, Münchner Germanistische Beiträge, Bd. 33 (Munich: Fink, 1986), 102-105.

Serenus to fire a few parting salvos of his customary derogatory arsenal at the violin concerto, "'the apotheosis of salon music'" (410/VI 544). This comment, addressed to Adrian himself, only elicits an enigmatic smile from the composer in response.

Parody is also in evidence in the second and central movement, appropriately labeled a "scherzo." In a manner "half-respectful, half caricature" (410/VI 544), the score calls for the emulation of the bowing techniques of such predecessors as Vieuxtemps and Wieniawski, composers who, although not exactly "lightweights" in the arena of the musical history, still cannot be ranked among the giants in the repertoire of violin literature. Even the inordinately long "gestation period" for this work — five years — might be indicative of the difficulties encountered by a composer compromising his standards. In accordance with Rudi's initial proposition to Adrian (the ambivalence of the English term "proposition" between sexual inference and the aesthetic intent is appropriate to the situation), the second movement could contain a distinctly modern form of parody: a musical quotation from Tartini's "Devil's Trill" Sonata. This device places a "devilishly difficult" bit of virtuoso musicianship from an earlier age at the center of an aesthetic artifact of the twentieth century. The novel *Doctor Faustus* itself is a modern creation having at its core and midpoint a *tour de force* dialogue with a diabolic figure, written in devilishly difficult antiquated style from past centuries, thereby evincing verbal virtuosity of a marked degree. Of course, the entire work is a parodic (and sometimes parodistic) version of the sixteenth-century chapbook. Parody serves as both subject and as object in this novel.

Almost as if to confirm his diagnosis of the frivolity of the concerto and to insure that posterity will be in accord with his biased assessment, Serenus follows the analysis of the composition with a discussion of salon music in the Munich circles. This constitutes art and artistry with, at best, surface or superficial appeal — or so he conjectures. At one of the soirées at the home of the industrialist Bullinger, waltzes from Gounod's *Faust* (not an insignificant title in the context of this novel) as well as those by Johann Strauß and Josef Lanner are played on the gramophone. Baptist Spengler, the syphilitic "Esmeraldus," now in wretched health due to the ravages of the disease, engages in an animated discussion with Leverkühn. Spengler attacks this music as drawing-room imitation of real folk dances. To the surprise of everyone, however, Adrian refuses to speak derogatorily of such popular pieces, because he had a teacher of music who was "too much in love with every ... organized noise ... for me to have learned any contempt from him. There was no such thing as being 'too good' for any sort of music" (412/VI 547).

As if to illustrate how this teacher inculcated a love for any organized sound in the student, Adrian requests a recording of Delilah's aria from Saint-

Saëns, *Samson et Dalila*. This was a work for which Kretzschmar, although a "fugue-man" at heart, nevertheless "had a peculiarly passionate feeling" (413/VI 548). The phonograph record of this old war horse is, indeed, located. Soon *"Mon coeur s'ouvre à ta voix"* pours forth, revealing a strophic-melodic contour which threatens to overpower the senses, especially when the "voluptuous vocal line" is accompanied by the violin (413/VI 548). Surreptitiously, Mann has smuggled into the fictional fabric a foreshadowing of the ménage à trois between Leverkühn (of Samsonesque stature in the musical world), Delilah (Marie Godeau, who "betrays" the hero of the Hebrews to the Philistines), and Schwerdtfeger (the producer of a "voluptuous" violin tone which pleases the philistine masses). Therefore, with *Samson* (as previously with *Faust*) another opera-cipher enters the bevy of actual compositions (*Tristan und Isolde, Salomé, Don Giovanni*), augmented by an array of fictitious operatic works (*Das Marmorbild, Love's Labour's Lost*), which can serve as shorthand symbols for the interplay of music, love, and death.

Leverkühn, arguing with Spengler in a fashion which suggests a deviation from his usual quest for objectivity through the application of the intellect, seems to have become a most articulate spokesman for the sensuous appeal of salon music. He maintains quite uncharacteristically: "the mind and spirit are by no means addressed by the spiritual alone; they can be most deeply moved by the animal sadness of sensual beauty. They have even paid homage to frivolity" (414/VI 549). If anyone, then Adrian Leverkühn ought to know the validity of this statement. It is a kind of veiled allusion, this time not to future events, but to his own "frivolity" with Hetæra. Hence the significance of his addendum: "Philine, after all, is nothing but a little strumpet, but Wilhelm Meister, who is not so very different from his creator, pays her a respect in which the vulgarity of innocent sensuality is openly denied" (414/VI 549). Has not another "master," Adrian Leverkühn, paid homage to a "little strumpet" himself and then, nullified the vulgar potential of such crass sensuality?

Adrian's crowning comment during this disquisition on morality in art in general and music in particular is not only applicable to his present frame of mind but also to the framework into which he sets his later compositions — especially his last work. "What becomes," he asks rhetorically, "of the whole jingle-jangle if you apply the most rigorously intellectual standards? A few 'pure spectra' of Bach. Perhaps nothing else audible would survive at all" (414/VI 550). These rather cryptic remarks anticipate the closing comment of Serenus Zeitblom on the *Dr. Fausti Weheklag*, as he searches for a resolution to his own dilemma when confronted with a similar artistic paradox. Pondering the mystery of how pure constructiveness can yield expressiveness, Serenus muses: "may we not parallel with it [this paradox] another, a religious one, and say too (though only in the lowest whisper) that out of the sheerly irremediable hope might germinate?" (491/VI 651).

Zeitblom, who by his own admission, can only treat "the phenomenon of love" analytically, dryly and stiffly (415/VI 550), nevertheless gains new insights in the course of the salon music debate. He discovers a connecting link between Adrian's sudden acquiescence to music of an inferior aesthetic quality (popular waltzes and *Samson*) and the violin concerto written for Rudi, "for whom it represented a conquest in more than in one sense of the word" (415/VI 550). Obviously the violinist remains totally oblivious to these "signs of ironic eroticism" (415/VI 550) in the music which secretly delighted Serenus.[8] The concerto takes both father (composer) and mother (soloist) to the Vienna premiere of the work. From there they journey to the estate of the absent Frau von Tolna in Hungary where, in spite of Adrian's persistent headaches, the homosexual relationship is consummated. The ironic inversion of the normal heterosexual sequence of procreation (impregnation, conception, birth) should not escape our attention.

The twosome later travels together to Switzerland in order to introduce their mutually conceived offspring to a wider public. Even though critics there find "a certain lack of unity in the style, ... in the level of the composition" (417/VI 553), as Serenus reports blandly but with secret satisfaction, the composer does appear on stage "hand in hand" with Rudi to receive the kudos of the audience. The gesture of holding hands with another individual had been a rarity in Adrian's life. It was restricted later to Jeanette Scheurl (who, as usual, had also made a pilgrimage to Berne for the concert), to his surrogate mother, Mrs. Schweigestill in Pfeiffering and to Nepomuk Schneidewein, the divine child and Adrian's "last love." There is a touch of situational irony as well as "ironic eroticism" in the fact that, during this moment of aesthetic triumph in Berne and Zurich, following closely on the heels of their homosexual adventure in Hungary, Adrian and Rudi meet Marie Godeau. This is the woman who, by her sheer femininity, will not only undermine the homoerotic ties between them, but also pave the way for Rudi's death and help prepare the path for Adrian's ultimate spiritual demise through collusion in the destruction of his friend.

With the advent of Marie Godeau, the one-time marriage à deux becomes a curious ménage à trois (actually "à quatre"), the complex, polyphonic nature of which gives rise to *liaisons dangereuses*. Marie's family name has acoustical properties akin to the enigmatic "Godot" in Samuel

---

[8]For a good discussion of Mann's view on the necessarily ironic nature of the erotic when the intellect is exposed to love, see Hirschbach, *The Arrow and the Lyre*, 158-59.

Beckett's later stage success, a potentially "god"-like figure for whom the other characters are perennially waiting.[9] Her given name, by the same token, evokes associations with the Virgin intercessor and mediator between God and man. These outer indications are therefore propitious, implying that with Marie Godot, a form of love might evolve which holds a redeeming potential for Leverkühn. The milieu in which the Leverkühn-Godeau-Schwerdtfeger love triangle (or quadrangle, since Inez Rodde later enters the picture) has its roots is not a plush Munich salon, but rather the drawing room of a wealthy Zurich patron of the arts. The musical setting is already somewhat bizarre, since the host is an amateur cellist with a glass eye, who insists upon playing the gallant swain to his invited prima donnas and soubrettes (418/VI 554).

By chance or design of fate, Adrian sits at table next to Marie and listens enraptured to her "singing voice" (420/VI 558), which, in its warmth and timbre color not only resembles, but actually seems to be that of his mother. Since Marie is a set designer for certain Parisian opera houses and vaudeville theaters, Adrian conducts an animated conversation with her about the stage settings of such works as Ravel's *Daphnis et Chloé* and Cimarosa's *Il matrimonio segretto*. These are operas which, because of their respective themes — the awakening of love and the propitious union of two lovers — do not seem to constitute merely random selections for discussion, but rather choices dictated by the conscious or even subconscious mind of the participants.

When Adrian subsequently begins dropping hints to Serenus about his desire to terminate his hermitlike, hermetically sealed existence, the friend is inwardly overjoyed at the prospect. He surmises that this portends the dissolution of the "dissolute" bond with Schwerdtfeger. Serenus, in spite of his long-standing reservations about Adrian's ability to establish a love-relationship with the opposite sex ("Against my will, I doubted whether this man was made to win love of women" [422/VI 560]), begins to alter his opinion. A glance at Marie convinces him that with this particular individual a unique musico-erotic bond might be possible for Adrian: "Did he not love her out of his own world of musical theology, oratorio, mathematical number-magic?" (423/VI 561). To Serenus and perhaps to the reader also, it begins to appear as though Adrian had been "waiting for Godeau" all along.

[9]Samuel Beckett's *Waiting for Godot* appeared in 1953.

An early indication of Adrian's need for "proxy representation"[10] in the quest to win Marie's favor is the proposal, quite out of character for him and more likely Schwerdtfeger's idea, that a group of friends take a sight-seeing excursion to the Bavarian fairy-tale castles of King Ludwig II. Serenus' musing suspicion on the subject leads him to interesting speculations: "Was the idea really Schwerdtfeger's, or had Adrian merely put it off on him out of shyness at assuming quite contrary to his nature the role of a lover... ?" (426/VI 565). On the train to Southern Bavaria, Adrian lavishes such praise on Rudi's playing that the violinist cannot refrain from a gesture in response to this warm admiration (as well as to other, more deep-seated inclinations): "And he pressed Adrian's knee. He was one of those people who always have to touch and feel — the arm, the shoulder, the elbow. He did it even to me, and also to women, most of whom did not dislike it" (428/VI 568).

On that evening prior to their tour of Bavaria's various architectural landmarks, the travelers spend a few hours at an inn with an illuminated dance floor. Rudi snatches the violin from a player in the orchestra and improvises magnificently, interspersing snippets "from the cadenza of 'his' concerto" (429/VI 569) with an impromptu rendition of Dvorák's "Humoresque." At this point, some of the incongruous "humor" of the entire enterprise manifests itself. The bisexual artist performing selections from a work conceived by him and his male partner, for the purpose of impressing a third party, Marie Godeau, the woman with whom each of the erstwhile male lovers is now, in his own, unique fashion, heterosexually infatuated.

Some disturbing premonitions are stirred when the entourage visits a castle of "mad" King Ludwig II and engages in an animated debate on insanity and the escape from this condition through death. Serenus, by arguing against Rudi's condemnation of both premises (madness and its termination in death), has the feeling of serving as Adrian's proxy, his "mouthpiece," so to speak, for the benefit of Marie. Once more the topic of "wooing" for another, a theme which will subsequently come to dominate and ultimately detonate an explosive double Tristanesque love triangle, comes to the fore. In the ensuing dénouement, Rudi functions as the ineptly apt Tantris-Tristan, pleading half-heartedly to a reluctant Isolde (Marie) the cause of a musical Marke (Adrian). Rudi becomes himself the involuntary pawn, the "marked man," so to speak, in a subsidiary power struggle between another strong-willed Isolde (Inez Rodde) and her pedestrian husband (Helmut Institoris).

[10]Cerf, in "The Shakespearean Element," 430-41, following the lead of Frank Harris' *The Man Shakespeare* (a source work actually used by Thomas Mann while writing *Doctor Faustus*) traces the roots of the wooing by proxy motif from its Shakespearean origin to its Mannian variations in the novel.

During the spring thaw in the period after the Bavarian sojourn, Adrian summons "the companion of his Hungarian journey" (434/VI 576) to Pfeiffering. Serenus' nasty circumlocution for Rudi is particularly cutting at this point, since it reminds the reader of the ulterior motive behind (or ultimate result of) the trip taken by composer and virtuoso: the consummation of a homosexual liaison. Conversely, by devious inference, it also alludes to the results of an earlier "musical" trip to the city of Pressburg in the Austro-Hungarian Empire, the consummation of which was a heterosexual relationship.

One day at the Schweigestill farm, Adrian and Rudi stroll around the Klammer Pond (the Pfeiffering counterpart to the body of water at Buchel known as the Cow Trough, both of which, because of their concave form and function, could serve as female symbols for Freudian interpreters). The composer and his companion engage in some not entirely insignificant "shop talk" about the upcoming music program that evening in Munich. Almost in passing Adrian introduces the topic of a need for human warmth — the kind of bovine warmth exuded by Hanne, the stable maid, during her canon singing years ago — something which, up to now, only the violinist and his warm friendship had given the composer: "A man came into my life; by his heartfelt holding out he overcame death — you might really put it like that. He released the human in me, taught me happiness" (437/VI 579). And by dint of the persistence of this individual — Rudi, of course, is the "man" in question — Adrian was able to conquer the kind of spiritual atrophy in which he was mired at the time. It is this same Rudi whom Adrian now selects as his emissary and intermediary to ask for Marie's hand in marriage: "I thought of you for this service of love because you would be much more in your element than, let us say, Serenus Zeitblom" (439-440/VI 583-584). Thus we have the strange situation of Adrian trying to convert a homosexual "vice" into a heterosexual "virtue," a proposal for proxy representation which Leverkühn readily equates with a stroke of musical inventiveness: "It is an idea of mine, an inspiration, the way something comes when you compose" (437/VI 581). Leverkühn's image may not be so out of place, if he is referring to that kind of compositional strategy which, while operating with virtual mathematical calculation, engenders, almost as a necessary by-product or corollary, its antithesis — emotional expressiveness. A similar dialectic will prevail in the proxy gambit: an erotic intrigue constructed with the calculated artistry of a musical composition will turn on an axis of diatonic interplay, into its diametrical opposite, emotional expressiveness. This, however, will not benefit the "composer" of the message, but rather the *Rosenkavalier*-like messenger, the medium, that is, through which the message is delivered.

Rudi's tactics to extricate himself from this mission of wooing for Adrian avail him little when, in desperation, he suggests Serenus as an alternative: "In my eyes," the composer counters, "he has nothing to do with love-affairs ..." (438/VI 582). Leverkühn is even able to brush off with apparent equanimity the violinist's startling confession of his own feelings for Marie and the fact that he (Rudi) had already committed a kind of aesthetic indiscretion: "Even in Zürich — after I had played, I had played *you* and was feeling warm and susceptible, she already charmed me" (439/VI 583). Leverkühn remains unflustered and, with an almost masochistic persistence,[11] reaffirms his choice of Rudi as they pass the hill known as Rohmbühel. This familiar landmark, because of its convex contours, could, like its parallel Mount Zion in Buchel, have phallic or perhaps even mammiform implications according to the psychoanalytic predisposition of the interpreter. Even though the designation Rohmbühel comes directly from the Dr. Faustus chapbook, the sheer frequency of allusions to this topographical feature (and to that of its Buchel counterpart, Mount Zion) suggests the author attributed more significance to it than mere fidelity to source material. Even Rudi's confession of love for Marie does not deter Leverkühn from his plan: "You will speak out of your own feelings, for me and my hopes. I cannot possibly think of a more ordained or desirable wooer" (440/VI 584). This becomes, however, a labor of love "lost" from its inception, as Serenus notes unceremoniously: "He had lost friend and beloved at one blow" (441/VI 586). The Thanatos factor intrudes into this ludicrous love triangle from a quarter as distorted as has been the entire Leverkühn-Godeau-Schwerdtfeger affair from the outset: Inez Rodde. This woman, who had once warned Adrian that Rudi "wanted everything," now intervenes and, herself, "goes all the way."

Naturally when a young man of "undeniable sexual appeal" (442/VI 586), a "fanatical male coquette" (442/VI 587), woos for another, he loses for his proxy but wins for himself, almost by proxy, one might say. In spite of Serenus' lack of experience in the erotic sphere, he appreciates the existential dilemma and human drama involved here: "how does one reveal to a woman that another man loves her?" (443/VI 588). Serenus also verbalizes the unique aesthetic-erotic dialectic: "the violin concerto was dedicated to him [Rudi], but

---

[11]Mann, in *Dichter über ihre Dichtungen* III, 142, notes in this connection: "He [Adrian] sent Rudi to his death, however, because he loved him. This is a murder required by the devil, because Adrian knows very well of the tension between Inez and Rudi." In another remark (144) from 1948, the author comments with regard to Leverkühn: "His belief in the possibility of Marie's love for him is very weak. He also knows that because of the devil's prohibition he cannot marry. He actually sends his friend to his death, that's the way it was conceived. He must do it, because love is forbidden him."

in the end it had been the medium of the composer's meeting with her [Marie]" (444/VI 589). One can certainly speak of erotic irony here, even though Mann himself had a much more complex and subtle view of what this concept entailed.

The proxy nature of Rudolf's original mission leads Serenus to suspect possible subterfuge on the part of the emissary from the outset:

> Rudolf repeated his wooing, only this time not for Adrian but himself. Of course, the feather-headed youth was as suited to the married state as I am to the role of Don Juan.... Marie had dared to love the breaker of hearts, the fiddler with the "little tone," whose artistic gifts and certain success had been vouched for to her by so weighty an authority. (445/VI 591)

The venom of vindictiveness which Serenus pours into such assessments is not even tempered by his foreknowledge of the outcome of this ill-fated liaison: "But it is idle to speculate on the chances for future happiness of a union doomed to no future at all, destined to be brought to naught by a violent blow from the hand of fate" (445/VI 591). The predestined force which puts an ignominious end to this enterprise has nothing to do with the fact that the breaker of hearts with the "little tone" is as much a marriage misfit as Serenus himself would be a miscast Don Juan. Instead, the "violent blow" comes from the intercession of an outside agent as insane and as inane, as warped and as weird as had been the Leverkühn-Godeau-Schwerdtfeger triple alliance from the start. Needless to say, Rudi's demise at the hand of the love-crazed Inez is totally devoid of any sense of a musically transfigured, Tristanesque love-death. Instead, it is portrayed as a scene of blood and gore, described with frighteningly dispassionate objectivity by Serenus, who happened to be among the eye-witnesses in the Munich streetcar.

After performing what was prophetically labeled his "farewell" concert in Munich prior to departing on a honeymoon with Marie, his bride-to-be, Rudi boards the tram to Schwabing. He sits unobtrusively among the other passengers, instrument case between his knees (another phallic symbol befitting a "Schwerdtfeger"). Suddenly, he is unceremoniously shot to death in cold blood by the insanely jealous Inez Rodde, the mistress whom he reluctantly accommodated and whom he was about to abandon for Marie. Inez' own husband, a Renaissance aesthetician and advocate of brute strength, had not only been branded "unmusical" (446/VI 592) but also unfeeling, so that Inez easily fell prey to the allure of the blue-eyed virtuoso. In fact, Serenus speculates on the irony that even this "manikin" (289/VI 384: "das Männchen") named Institoris unwittingly functioned as a "proxy wooer." Had he never wooed and won Inez in the first place, she would not have been driven into the arms of the other proxy wooer, Schwerdtfeger:

> ... Dr. Helmut approached her, as man to woman, and began to woo her. I was and remain convinced that Inez would never have fallen in love with Schwerdtfeger without the entry of Institoris into her life. He wooed her, but in a sense for another. A man not passionate himself could by his courtship and the trains of thought connected with it arouse the woman in her.... (296/VI 395)

Serenus further conjectures, not without a touch of "sour grapes," that it was music which aided and abetted the cause of the erotic in the case of the Schwerdtfeger-Inez affair:

> Compared with Institoris, who was a mere instructor in the beautiful, Rudolf had on his side the advantage of art at first hand: art, nourisher of the passions, transcender of the human. For by his art the person of the beloved is elevated, from art the emotions ever draw fresh food, when the artist's own individuality is associated with the joys his art purveys. (297/VI 396)

In a literally "melo-dramatic" fashion, however, the triadic configuration, with the musician caught between the "devil and the deep blue sea," between Inez-Rodde-Institoris and Marie Godeau, culminates in an erotic-thanatotic tragedy deprived of any force of mitigation not to mention an aura of transcendence. The blue-eyed virtuoso, who lived by the perilous sword of proxy wooing, perished by that sword: and "Schwerdt-feger" was his name.

Conspicuously absent from the catalogue of Leverkühn's compositions to which an individual, prominent in his dealings with the social circles of Munich, contributes some intrinsic or even extrinsic element, is any musical work inspired by Marie Godeau. She is the one woman with whom Adrian sought to establish something resembling a "normal" relationship. Perhaps the very aspect of normalcy entailing a period of courtship (which, in this case, was to be anything but routine), followed by a formal wedding ceremony and a life of marital obligation, precluded the transcription of these prospects into the heart and soul of Leverkühn's innovative music.

The texts and tales from which his music was derived were invariably out of the ordinary, even extra-ordinary, as, for instance, the later discussion of the *Gesta Romanorum* will show. On the other hand, it could be argued that elements of the tragicomic misadventure with Marie had already been prefigured in Leverkühn's opera, that genre which has supplied so many shorthand ciphers for the Melos-Eros-Thanatos configuration. In this case, the title alone says it all: *Love's Labour's Lost*. By the same token, certain premonitions of the double love-triangle (Adrian—Marie—Rudi : Rudi—Inez —Institoris) find expression in other literary works with Shakespearean background which command his interest. This is especially true of those in which erotic triple ententes abound: the Sonnets and *Twelfth Night* come to mind.[12]

The completion and premiere of the opera (1915) postdate Adrian's Hetæra Esmeralda experience by a decade (1905). One might, therefore, expect to find reminiscences of that affair in this work. By the same token, even though *Love's Labour's Lost* and its "decimating music" (263/VI 349) antedate Adrian's encounter with Marie Godeau by about ten years, much of the ambience of the piece foreshadows what was to happen later in life. No sooner did Adrian return from his mission in Pressburg and undergo that unsuccessful medical treatment (1906), than he confirmed his intention of writing an opera based on Shakespeare's "conceited comedie" of ca. 1594. This was a play with which critics have dealt harshly and which commentators have handled not so much with kid gloves as with benign neglect.[13] The details of the origin and evolution of Adrian's setting of the comedy are scattered throughout approximately 100 pages of the text, culminating with the unsuccessful first performance of the work in Lübeck.

As a kind of preliminary exercise to composing an opera which entails "a marriage of the media,"[14] Adrian honed his skills in the musico-poetic amalgam of the lied, by setting German, Italian, French and English lyrics to music. These were not merely randomly selected texts, but rather poems chosen with the confluence of Melos-Eros-Thanatos in mind. The genre of the lyric song was by no means new to Leverkühn. Kretzschmar, it will be recalled, had once introduced him to the theory of the lied via Schumann's settings of

[12]Cerf, "The Shakespearean Element," 428-29.

[13]*Love's Labour's Lost*, ed. John Dover Wilson (Cambridge, England: Cambridge University Press, 1969), "Introduction," xxiv.

[14]Sommerhage, *Eros und Poesis*, 259, speaking of art (music) as a form of sexual sublimation for the artist and of the art work as his sort of compensatory beloved, uses sexually explicit imagery as a hermeneutic principle ("mating of the contradictory," "the erotic conquest of the contrast of contrasts") to indicate the manner in which the aesthetic artifact achieves the fusion or union of such apparent opposites as subject-object, the serious and the comic, etc. (in this connection, see especially 265 ff.)

Eichendorff. The musicalization of Brentano's daring lyric songs and ballads in the radically new musical idiom utilizing the five-note signature theme have already been discussed in some detail.[15] At the more ethereal end of the spectrum were Leverkühn's settings of lyrical sections from Dante's *Divine Comedy*, especially the lines showing the poet illuminated by the light of the planet Venus. The musical texture is characterized by an interweaving or intertwining "embrace" of the voices (162/VI 216).

Leverkühn's songs based on French and English poetry incorporate elements of the erotic much less sidereal and more terrestrial; in fact, some are quite "down to earth," even "earthy." Verlaine's "Un grand sommeil noir/ Tombe sur ma vie" and his macabre invitation "Mourons ensemble, voulez vous?" all contain the seeds of a budding love-death constellation, transposed, to be sure, to a something less than exalted context. It is, however, William Blake's lyrics which are most incisive in capturing graphically the full impact of the love-death liaison. Echoes of the Hetæra Esmeralda-Leverkühn situation re-sound here when we read of the sick rose, "whose life was destroyed by the dark secret love of the worm which found its way into her crimson bed" (165/VI 220). The diseased flower ("Rose, thou art sick") serves as an ominous reminder of the venereal infection coursing osmotically through Adrian's system and moving inexorably toward the brain. The stealthy worm is a distant relative of the serpent and its toxicity. The crimson bed of love might be compared with the rouged "carmine-red" cheeks of the Leipzig prostitute who confronted and confounded Adrian, compelling him to seek refuge at the piano.

These were the Blake settings from Leverkühn's early Leipzig years (1905-1910). Yet even when he returns to the same English poet some time later, the force of attraction is still the subtle, shocking subject matter. He continues to be held spellbound by the orbit of Esmeralda, as the closing couplet from "Silent, Silent Night" indicates: here we learn how an honest joy "Does itself destroy / For a harlot coy" (263/VI 350). Even more startling than the Hetæra-oriented imagery is the musical setting which utilizes a principle that becomes endemic to his late style of composing:

> These darkly shocking verses the composer had set to very simple harmonies, which in relation to the tone-language of the whole, had a "falser," more heart-rent, uncanny effect than the most daring harmonic tensions and made one actually experience the common chord growing monstrous. (263-264/VI 350)

[15]For an analysis of the entire cycle of Brentano songs, see John Fetzer, "Clemens Brentano's Muse and Adrian Leverkühn's Music: Selective Affinities in Thomas Mann's *Doktor Faustus*," *Essays in Literature* 7 (1980): 115-31.

The device of employing a conventional musical texture to strengthen highly unconventional poetic contexts becomes a trademark of Leverkühn's evolving technique. It had characterized the Brentano songs and it subsequently resurfaces as the hallmark of his comic opera *Love's Labour's Lost*.

The driving force behind the adaptation of this work in its English original during the years from approximately 1910 to 1914 was Adrian's erstwhile mentor, Wendell Kretzschmar. The subject matter of the latter's own opera, *The Marble Statue*, the source of which might have been either Eichendorff or Andersen, revealed that the erotically tinged aesthetic artifact was of no mean importance to this mentor. And it has already been documented that the teacher represents "the personified conscience of the pupil." A second noteworthy circumstance surrounding Adrian's opera is that it shares the fate of another initially unsuccessful venture, Debussy's *Pelléas et Mélisande*. Serenus is careful to note that at the Munich premiere of *Pelléas* in 1907, two-thirds of the audience reputedly left the theater during the performance. In this respect, Adrian is keeping good company. As one has come to expect in Mann's oeuvre, however, even the choice of this predecessor in failure is not fortuitous, but rather carefully calculated. A close examination of the text of *Pelléas*, for instance, reveals that it is a work in which music, love, and death figure prominently in a triangular relationship which anticipates Adrian's later plight with Rudi: the woman between two rival suitors. A further element worth noting in conjunction with the premiere is that a lone critic with a crabbed, old-fashioned writing style was the only positive voice in the wilderness. Amid a welter of adverse reaction to the "decimating" score, he acknowledged Leverkühn's opus as a "work of the future, full of profound music" (263/VI 350). His addendum that the composer was both a "mocker" as well as "a 'god-witted' man" (263/VI 350) underscores attributes of reciprocity which, in Adrian's case, are both complementary and complimentary.

From the very conception of this opera to its ultimate conclusion, the marriage of the media — verbal and vocal — together with the themes of love and marriage had been prime concerns.[16] "Music and speech, he insisted,

---

[16]It is interesting to note that all of Leverkühn's major works involve the interplay of text and tones in some fashion. This even holds — metaphorically, at least — for the cluster of pure chamber works of 1927, each of which has literary affiliations. The ensemble for strings, woodwinds and piano, for instance, is a "discursive piece" concerning which Adrian maintains he did not want to write " 'a sonata but a novel' " (456/VI 605). The high point of this "tendency to musical prose" is the string quartet of the same year. The only composition of Adrian which did not have specific links to literature was the juvenile *Meeresleuchten*, written in the derivative, "dead-tooth" style of the Impressionists, and even this could be categorized

belonged together, they were at bottom one, language was music, music a language; separate, one always appealed to the other, imitated the other, used the other's tools, always one gave itself to be understood as substitute of the other" (163/VI 217). This intimate union had been in evidence in the Brentano songs and remained so in Adrian's settings of other lyrics (an activity which, as previously indicated, he considered a "practice for a complete work in words ' and music which hovered before his mind's eye" [163/VI 217]). Two large-scale paradigms for this fusion of tone and text in the future were Wagner's "word-tone drama" (164/VI 218) and Beethoven's Ninth Symphony. In a sense, *Love's Labour's Lost* with its persiflage of the erotic sphere represents a kind of "taking back" of *Tristan und Isolde*, while Leverkühn's *Lamentation of Dr. Faustus* is specifically designated as an attempt to "take back' the "joy" and euphoria of the Ninth.

The intimate alliance of plot and musical score also extends to the thematic substance of the work,[17] which Adrian treats in as un-Wagnerian, anti-Tristanesque a manner as possible. Not only does the play represent a persiflage of artificial behavior in matters of human heart and amorous situations, but it also becomes a parody of the persiflage of the artificial. This is accomplished by the juxtaposition of "the lout and 'natural' alongside the comic sublime," causing both to appear "ridiculous in each other" (164/VI 218).[18] Adrian's original librettist had been Rüdiger Schildknapp, whose name in its etymological components harks back to the age of medieval chivalry, that kind of "artificial" code of stylized Minne and courtly morals which this ultra-modern opera bouffe is intended to parody. Bantering back and forth with Rüdiger, the composer focuses on what he conceived as the quintessential feature of the work: "the fool's cap of passion" (164/VI 219), in

as a kind of "program music."

[17]The rather thin plot of *Love's Labour's Lost*, summarized in all brevity, deals with the arbitrary resolve of King Ferdinand of Navarre and his three attendants including Biron of Berowne, to foreswear worldly and social pleasures (above all the companionship of women) for three years. During this period of enforced abstinence, they intend to devote themselves to serious study and meditation. No sooner have they made their decision, when the Princess of France arrives on state business with her entourage, which includes Rosaline and two other handmaidens. Needless to say, the charms of the female quartet soon break down the will-power of the four men, and one by one the latter seek and win the favor of their respective ladies. But the women put them to the acid test of a year's probation and fidelity: if, at the end of twelve months, the suitors are still as ardent and adamant in their pleas, the ladies might be persuaded to entertain a marriage proposal.

[18]Cerf, "The Shakespearean Element," 434.

other words, the manner in which highly charged emotion unmasks the learned man. Nothing burns with such a torrid flame as "'gravity's revolt to wantonness'" (164/VI 219), as Shakespeare phrased it and as Leverkühn, if anybody, should know in the light of his brief encounter with the elemental force of Hetæra Esmeralda.

The composer assumes an equivocal stance in his tonal setting of the libretto (and in terms of the German title of the novel, he *is* a "Tonsetzer"): "only too well did Adrian's music see to it that in the end feeling came no better off than the arrogant forswearing of it" (217/VI 289). By this means Leverkühn could create something which was both "true to life" (his personal revolt to wantonness) and "true to art" (the aesthetic transformation of the promiscuous woman and even the prostitute in the works of the Romantics and post-romantic generations). In addition, his later gravitation toward another lifestyle which a Marie Godeau might hold in store for him is also foreshadowed here: "disparate forms of a cocoonlike withdrawal from the world and an inward need of world-wideness" (165/VI 220).

A key facet of *Love's Labour's Lost* is articulated in a frank discussion after the wedding (1910) of Ursula Leverkühn to the upright Swiss, Johannes Schneidewein. Adrian, a reluctant attendant at this "sacrificial feast of a maidenhead" (186/VI 248) and suffering from nagging headaches, pontificates to Serenus on how the Christian sacrament of marriage merely sanctifies the carnal element of sexual passion. This standpoint disturbs Serenus, especially because of his own intention to enter the honorable state of matrimony. An exchange of quotations from the comedy ensues, in which frivolous elements of love and death are tossed about: "But, if thou marry, hang me by the neck, if horns that year miscarry!" (188/VI 251). Goaded on by Serenus' repartee, Adrian begins to expound on his evolving conception of the "strict style," arguing in spite of persistent head pains (190-91/VI 255) that "Organization is everything." Previously, it should be mentioned, "relationship" in the form of ambiguity, had been the mainstay of music. Just what that ultimate organization will entail emerges in skeletal and theoretical form on this occasion; the requisites for the "total integration" will only be forthcoming at the end of Leverkühn's creative life with his *Weheklag* (1930). Noteworthy, however, is the fact that the theory of the "strict style" is conceived amid an intense discussion of love and sex. Then, only after a long gestation period, do the seeds of that intellectual conception bear fruit when Leverkühn's last and greatest work is born.

In Italy one year later (1911), just prior to reading Kierkegaard's exposé of *Don Giovanni* and the musical erotic, and immediately preceding the encounter with the impudent interlocutor, Adrian refines his compositional strategies for the comic opera even further. The juxtaposition of the "natural" and the "comic sublime" in the melodic-erotic-thanatotic framework crystallizes for him when he composes music for such lines as : "'By the Lord, this love is as mad as Ajax; it kills sheep; it kills me, I am a sheep'" (215/VI 287). When justifying the musical technique of repetition, Leverkühn enumerates a fundamental concept which also holds true for this novel in general and for the music-love-death constellation in particular: "in music, the repetition of the significant and already familiar, the suggestive or subtle invention, always makes the strongest and most speaking impression" (215/VI 287). As if to underscore the impact of repetition (and variation) in an aesthetic context, the seminal excerpt about the revolt of gravity to wantonness is now quoted in full and in German: "Der Jugend Blut brennt nicht mit solcher Glut,/ Als Ernst, einmal empört zur Sinneswut" (VI 288). Whereas the inferences of this passage definitely point to the pursuit of Hetæra, the implications of the force of repetition apply both to her and to Marie Godeau. Adrian "repeated" his visit to Esmeralda, with all the consequences that entailed. Adrian sought through his proxy wooer, Rudi, to have someone "repeat" to the object of his affections the feelings which he himself was incapable of expressing directly: also with devastating results.

The portrayal of Rosaline "as a faithless, wanton, dangerous piece of female flesh" (216/VI 288) and the deliberate linkage of her with the "dark lady" of the Shakespearean sonnets (216/VI 288) also point to Hetæra. She was the "brown wench" (142/VI 191) who also proved to be a "dangerous piece of female flesh," inducing the "grave" Adrian to "revolt" against his previous ascetic modus vivendi. In spite of Serenus' deep-seated reservations about this theatrical persiflage of love, this "arrogant travesty" (218/VI 290), he still finds its music fascinating: "a tense, sustained, neck-breaking game played by art on the edge of impossibility" (218/VI 290). Because of the interpenetrability of what he terms "admiration and sadness, admiration and doubt" in the work, Zeitblom conjectures that it might almost serve "as the definition of love" (218/VI 290). It was the quality of artifice in art, together with the unmasking of the artificiality of the well-made artifact, which led the adversarial apparition in Italy to cite the out-moded diction of *Love's Labour's Lost* in order to defuse Adrian's arguments: "A clever artifice, an [sic] 'twere stolen from thine own opera! But we make no music here at the moment" (224-25/VI 299).

Upon his return to Pfeiffering from Italy, Leverkühn completes the score for this work, especially after locating a copyist who not only transcribes the work flawlessly, but also conveys through his transcription an appreciation for the complexity of the music. This individual, a bassoonist by trade, proves particularly adept in assessing the parodistic ambience at the core of the opera:

> Not enough could he admire the fine subtlety of the workman-
> ship, the versatile rhythms, the technique of instrumentation, by
> which an often considerable complication of parts was made
> perfectly clear; above all, the rich fantasy of the composition,
> showing itself in the manifold variations of a given theme. He
> instanced the beautiful and withal half-humorous music that
> belongs to the figure of Rosaline, or rather expresses Biron's
> desperate feeling for her.... (262/VI 348)

The tension between musical humor and emotional despair (Biron's love for Rosaline as a reflection of Adrian's Hetæra affair and/or as a precursor of Adrian's feelings for Marie?) becomes apparent in the bassoonist's analysis of the "tripartite bourrée" in the final act. This piece represents a revival of an antiquated French dance form refurbished with modern musical devices: "He added that this bourrée was not a little characteristic of the démodé archaic element of social conventionality which so charmingly but also so challengingly contrasted with the 'modern,' the free and more than free, the rebel parts, disdaining tonal connection, of the work" (262/VI 348). The confrontation and coalescence of dichotomous forces — social convention and rebellion against society — provides the necessary transfusion of life's blood to resuscitate lifeless forms. Their interplay in the opera and their common bond ("that in the end feeling came no better off than the arrogant foreswearing of it") reflect both Adrian's prior situation with the Hungarian prostitute (rebellion against society) as well as his subsequent involvement with the Swiss set designer (social convention).

The thrust of Shakespeare's "serious comedie" was directed against the foolishness of those who, by such artificially imposed injunctions as, in this case, the self-inflicted embargo against love, suppressed erotic emotions until the force of this elemental power caused a "break-through." At this point, they seek, in much too impetuous a fashion, to reinstate Eros to its proper place in the continuum of human intercourse. Adrian had always exuded a "Noli me tangere" air, implying "abstention from women" (220/VI 294), until "gravity's revolt to wantonness" took control and the "ethos of purity" was sacrificed to "the pathos of impurity" (220/VI 294). By the same token, his abrupt and unrealistic decision to woo and win Marie Godeau by "breaking through" his bachelor isolation and entering the state of matrimony has its precedent in the play. The comedy, however, closes with a kind of "checkmate" situation. The lady in question, too often deceived and disappointed by her once aloof and now ardent wooer, refuses to accept his offer of marriage without the penalty of probation. In fact, all potential matings in the play are frozen in a state of indefinite postponement, so that for the time being, at least, love's labors are, indeed, lost. Given what we already know about the "tripartite bourrée" and its function in Leverkühn's opera of juxtaposing social convention with anti-social, even anarchically unsocial elements, the fact that Rudi approaches Adrian whistling this selection "precisely in the right pitch" (349/VI 464) is striking. The epicene Rudi and the abstemious anchorite collaborate on their joint venture and produce what Schwerdtfeger wishes: a violin concerto. Somehow Rudi hopes through this music to extricate himself from his entanglement in an unbearable love triangle with Inez and her husband, but in the process he gets more than he bargained for. His emotional involvement with Adrian and their mutual musical offspring lead to a still more complicated triangular situation involving Adrian and Marie Godeau, one in which the reciprocity of the Melos-Eros-Thanatos components cannot be underestimated.

Musical Correlations: Beyond Good and Evil?

In conjunction with almost every major figure in the novel who enters the orbit of Adrian Leverkühn's universe, essential features of that personal interaction were incorporated, overtly, into the conception and execution of a major musical composition.[19] Human relations found their corresponding musical correlations. Hetæra Esmeralda became a five-note sequence in the Brentano song cycle (ca. 1906) and her signature motif, if we can accept Serenus' statements, haunted all of Adrian's subsequent works, culminating in the *Weheklag* (1930). The antinomic quality characteristic of the "O lieb Mädel" song also dominated the work most closely allied with Frau von Tolna (who, on the basis of considerable textual evidence, might be considered identical with Hetæra): the *Apocalypsis cum figuris* (1919). But in keeping with the incognito nature of von Tolna's ties to Adrian, this woman was neither "seen" nor "heard" in the composition itself — certainly not to the extent that Esmeralda had been. Rudi's violin concerto (1924), on the other hand, functioned as a perfect — perhaps all too perfect — "objective correlative" for the clandestine homoerotic liaison between creator and performer. This was not only due to the lilting signature themes, but also because of the overall tenor of the "salon" showpiece, its stylistic designations and blatant sensuous appeal. Finally, the opera *Love's Labour's Lost* (1915) both recapitulated elements of

---

[19]For the first systematic and general survey of Adrian's entire creative musical output, see Jack M. Stein, "Adrian Leverkühn as a Composer," *The Germanic Review* 25 (1950), 257-74. Most recently, there is the comprehensive investigation by Harald Wehrmann, *Thomas Manns 'Doktor Faustus'. Von den fiktiven Werken Adrian Leverkühns zur musikalischen Struktur des Romans*.

Adrian's response to his Esmeralda liaison and anticipated some of the idiosyncrasies of his subsequent mishandling of the Marie Godeau affair.

Marie Godeau never attains the status of those other females engendering a distinctive musical motif or stylistic profile in Adrian's compositions. But there is one shred of evidence, albeit speculative in nature, that this woman, like her namesake Maria in the realm of Catholicism, might have functioned as a mediating force between the apostate composer and some higher power. One could term the origins of this quality the "Ave Maria" syndrome (the Virgin Mother of the savior of mankind, Holy Mary as intercessor) as opposed to the original "sin" of "Eva" (temptation through the serpent to eat the apple from the tree of the Knowledge of Good and Evil, loss of Paradise); whereas the former redeems, the latter condemns. After all, the predominant letter symbol in Hetæra's motif had been an "e" ("h-e-a-e-es"), and this "e" could well stand for Eva, just as "h" and "es" stood for Hetæra and Esmeralda respectively. As the only repeated note in the miniature tone row, however, the "e" actually constitutes an infraction or improper element, musically speaking, for in the true twelve tone series, no note is permitted to repeat until all others have sounded.

But perhaps even more significant in the context of the vowel and consonant symbolism is Marie's family name, Godeau, and the musical and ethical implications stemming from the initial "g." Of course, in terms of the Faust tradition, one immediately thinks of Gretchen (Goethe uses the diminutive form in reference to Margarete). It is she who, aided by the force of love from above, proves to be the mediator between the striving hero and realms of ever higher destiny and activity. The designation one could apply to such a form of redemption would be "grace," a concept rendered in German by another "g" word, "Gnade." Such grace is something one cannot consciously vow to attain; one cannot force the issue, but rather hope, even beyond hopelessness, that the deity or Godhead ("Gott," "Gottheit") will be moved by the power of divine love (Caritas) to pardon ("Gnade") even the most unpardonable of sins.

The thesis on which the remainder of this interpretation dealing with the role of Melos-Eros-Thanatos in the novel rests is this: scattered throughout the text are a number of clues which suggest attributing to the tone "g" and/or to chordal progressions or melodic sequences built on this note of the musical scale, a positive value. The most significant of these is the fact that at the end of Leverkühn's last composition, the *Weheklag*, the final note we hear played on a single, isolated instrument is a high "g." In view of Serenus' extensive analysis of this phenomenon, it would not be amiss to interpret it as an expression of hope, if ever so slight, that transcendence to something better or higher through the power of divine grace may still be possible. Precedents exist in the text for ascribing an edifying value to "g." For example, at the moment of Adrian's initial confrontation with the "Eva" aspect of the infernal female in the Leipzig bordello, he struck a series of chords on the piano, a transition passage from B major to C major, patterned on the hermit's prayer near the end of Weber's *Der Freischütz*. Now we can appreciate the prayer of a "hermit" (the anchorite which Adrian was to become) as well as the progression from B (or "H" in German, the tonal initial and tonic key of Hetæra) to C via the "six-four chord on G" (142/VI 190). Musically speaking, this second inversion of the tonic chord of C major built on "g" engenders in the listener a feeling of incompleteness, a need for resolution back to the "tonic," a return to the tonal center (C major) from which one has deviated. The chord based on "g" would thus function as the connecting link back to the tonic after diversion to B (H). On the metaphoric level, then, this aspect of the brothel scene could be interpreted as a foreshadowing of what is to come: the apostate hermit, Adrian Leverkühn, after his revolt to wantonness (Hetæra), and his arrogant "falling away" from God, seeks his salvation through a reunion, in the same etymological sense that "re-ligio" infers,[20] with a higher spiritual entity in the universe. The mediating force in this process of reunification with divine love (the key of "C" signifying, perhaps, a form of Caritas) after having strayed into a diabolically inspired eroticism ("H" or Hetæra), would be some form of redeeming grace. The musical and letter symbol for this saving "grace" ("g") might have been incorporated in a figure such as Godeau. But this, like so many other potentially positive incidents in the novel, was simply "not to be" in Mann's subtle scheme of things. Yet in a novel in which the central concern is the arrogant apostasy from God of one who rejects theology and turns to demonology, it is not unusual that a host of terms would appear dealing with prayer ("Gebet"), faith ("Glaube") in God ("Gott"), the godhead ("die Gottheit"), grace ("Gnade"), goodness ("Güte"), and the like. This assumption is borne out in the course of the work.[21]

The sensually erotic, five-note tonal cipher for Hetæra had aroused a feeling of chromatic non-resolution akin to the restless, unresolved tensions of

---

[20]One frequently cited etymological explanation for the derivation of the word "religion," *Webster's Third New International Dictionary* (Chicago: Encyclopædia Britannica, 1966), 1918, points to the root element in "ligare" ("tying" as in "ligature"). This concept, together with the prefix "re," suggests that "religion," at least in its origins, dealt with an act of tying back again something that had broken loose.

[21]I developed this topic at length in a paper, *"Doktor Faustus* and the Music Mann: Adrian Leverkühn's Air for the G String," delivered at the International Symposium on "Music and German Literature," University of Illinois, Urbana-Champaign, April 1989.

Wagner's *Tristan* score. Leverkühn's last work, as will be demonstrated later, expands the five-note pattern to the maximum musical potential of a twelve-tone row, only to conclude with a single "g" sound played by a single cello. This minimalist reduction, almost an aesthetic *reductio ad absurdum*, represents the converse of the musical complexity previously encountered in this work and in Leverkühn's entire oeuvre. It signals his reversion to music's most primordial roots — unadulterated, untempered monody — after having run the full gamut of polyphony, harmony, a-tonality, polytonality, and dodecaphony. The fact that an isolated "g" resonates as the parting tonal legacy of his final work, and then only lingers on imperceptibly as "a light in the night" (491/VI 651), adds considerable weight to Adrian's previously quoted comment in the debate with the "Esmeraldus" Spengler over salon music: "What becomes of the whole jingle-jangle if you apply the most rigorously intellectual standards? ... Perhaps nothing else audible would survive at all" (414/VI 550).

Three additional instances of the role of the musical "g" as a symbolic potential for God's grace "beyond good and evil," might, perhaps, convince the still skeptical reader of the validity or at least applicability of this hypothesis. Leverkühn's vocal suite of dramatic grotesques for puppets entitled *Gesta Romanorum* (1915) treated a number of erotically tinged anecdotes from a medieval collection of salacious tales and fables, ranging from the comically ribald to the incestuous. Inspiration for this suite came from Kleist's essay on the marionettes, and Mann takes pains to mention many times in close context that Kleist was dealing with the loss of an attribute granted the puppet and God alone: "*G*razie, die eigentlich dem *G*liedermann und dem *G*otte ... vorbehalten ist" (308/VI 410, italics mine). This came about due to the "breakthrough" of consciousness in man. In this instance, the term used, "Grazie," is devoid of the religious connotation of "pardon," but certainly the "tonality" of the key consonant is sustained.

Illustrative of the category of the salacious in the *Gesta* is "Of Godless Guile," a humorous tale which recounts the fate of women who fail to comply with the sexual demands of their partners: they are transformed into weeping canines. With regard to the consonant symbolism under consideration here, it is important to note that the title of this immoral story, "Von der gottlosen List" (VI 464), contains the "g" sound in a kind of in absentia or ex negativo format: such calculated deceit is a form of "godlessness." But the moral implication is that one must scrupulously avoid such temptations and convert human cunning into its diametrical opposite: at best "godlikeness," or at least "goodness."

A more extreme instance of sexual perversion set in the context of a musical travesty in the *Gesta* is the story of Gregory, the "Holy Sinner" of the Middle Ages, the medieval Oedipus, whose fate seemed to seal his doom beyond hope of redemption. Gregory (another of those "g"-names), as the offspring of an illicit brother-sister liaison, compounds the felony of his parents by marrying his own mother. Learning of his unwitting yet sinful transgression, Gregory has himself chained to a rock in the sea, where he does penance for seventeen years. Having found "grace" through "faith" ("Gnade — Glaube") he is subsequently hailed as "Gregory, thou man of God" (319/VI 424), and ascends to the papacy.

Serenus, in a series of very perceptive remarks, notes that the *Gesta* embody a demontage of the type of the high-flown word-tone drama of redemption found in the ethos of the Wagnerian repertoire: Adrian's approach, on the other hand, represented

> travesty, springing as it did from a critical rebound after the swollen pomposity of an art epoch nearing its end. The musical drama had taken its materials from the romantic sagas, the myth-world of the Middle Ages, and thus suggested that only such subjects were worthy of music, or suited to its nature. Here [in the *Gesta*] the conclusion seemed to be drawn; in a right destructive way, indeed, in that the bizarre, and particularly the farcically erotic, takes the place of the moralizing and priestly, all inflated pomp of production is rejected and the action transferred to the puppet theatre, in itself already burlesque. (319-20/VI 425-26)

A typical scene in which the scurrilous, farcically erotic becomes a travesty of the pompously high moral seriousness of Wagnerian stamp is the Tristanesque episode in which the puppet figure portraying Gregory's mother covers the corpse of her beloved brother and brother-beloved with kisses from head to foot. Then, when the child of the ill-fated pair later meets and loves his own mother more than he should, the original sin of incest seems to have been magnified to such proportions that hope of redemption lies beyond all hope. But it is just this hope beyond hopelessness which triggers the mechanism of divine salvation.

Whereas it can be argued that the opera of 1915, *Love's Labour's Lost*, prefigured Adrian's situation with Marie Godeau only obliquely, the Pope Gregory section of this *Gesta romanorum* (1915) contains a twofold anticipation: both that of the composer's final and greatest work, the *Dr. Fausti Weheklag*, as well as his own fate. The compounding of the original infraction of incest in the *Gesta* is counterbalanced by the fact that the two "innocent" sinners find ultimate redemption. After confessing her sins to her son as Pope, Gregory's mother founds a cloister and remains its abbess until her death. This situation is interpreted as a sign that those guilty of even the basest of transgressions may still be saved: "The Devil thought to lead us to hell, but the greater power of God has prevented him" (319/VI 425). Mother and son are to be reconciled with God ("an Gott zurückzugeben" [319/VI 425]).

Obviously this kind of medieval morality play has a deep-seated message for Adrian. Already in the dialogue with the devil, faith in the *attritio cordis*, the idea that there exists a form of atonement for sin based on sincere repentance had been supplanted by *contritio cordis*. This latter doctrine derived from the conviction that there are infractions against the deity of such an egregious sort, that not even God's infinite mercy ("Gnadenakt") (VI 328) can forgive them. Only when the sinner reaches this low-water mark of utter despair can a glimmer of hope for pardon arise on the horizon. This was the ultimate form of "mercy" which the Holy Sinner Gregory was granted, and it survives as the only possible mode of redemption available to Adrian. However, as the adversary astutely points out, awareness of the very existence of forgiveness through *contritio cordis* brings with it a kind of invalidation of the premise.

Adrian Leverkühn's "last" love, that for his nephew Nepomuk Schneidewein, was literally a case of "love at first sight." This boy of five came to stay with him in 1928 in order to recuperate from recent illnesses. In the context of this relationship, especially in its later stages, "g" words designating God, Grace, Goodness, abound. When he first appears, the angelic lad, nicknamed "Echo," is adorned with such epithets by the adoring populace of Pfeiffering as: "a guest from some finer, tinier sphere" (461/VI 611), "the fairy princeling" (461/VI 611), or the "child of God" who had "dropped down from heaven" (464/VI 615). Particularly the last characterization deserves some careful scrutiny, not so much due to the key word and tonal cipher in "God," but rather to the concept of having "dropped down from heaven." Paradoxically, the act of falling calls to mind another figure who fell from heavenly grace only to become the leader of the hellish host: the former archangel Lucifer. Are there, one muses, grounds to suspect that the Great Adversary might also have a hand in the appearance of Adrian's "last love," just as he had been instrumental in orchestrating Leverkühn's first? In keeping with the acknowledged ties between the satanic and the erotic long ago underscored by the adversary in Italy, such subtle interconnections are not beyond the realm of possibility. One should add, for instance, that the planet Venus, celebrated in Dante's *Divine Comedy* as the morning star, also bears the designation "Lucifer" (perhaps more in the sense of "light bringer"), reconfirming a mysterious bond between sex and the diabolic. Potential luciferian ties between the heavenly Echo and the hellish host will be touched upon briefly after first establishing Nepo's close affinities with the Godhead.

There is nothing in the text to suggest that the avuncular love between Adrian and Nepo-Echo has the slightest trace of the sexual. On the contrary, it is the purest embodiment of a-sexual adoration, of love in its purest platonic form. As the virtual embodiment of divine perfection in his appearance, Echo is literally "too good to be true" — at least for this avowedly imperfect universe. Adrian is under the delusion that a mode of love directed toward such an ethereal creature, a form of bonding devoid of the sexual component, might not fall under the erotic ban imposed upon him by the "pact" with the adversary: "Love is forbidden you, in so far as it warms. Thy life shall be cold, therefore thou shalt love no human being" (249/VI 332). At the end of the brief interlude with Nepo, which ends so tragically, Adrian confesses his implication in the death of Rudi Schwerdtfeger in terms which, by extension, could even apply to the demise of his nephew:

> I had well thought before that I, as devil's disciple, might love in
> flesh and blood what was not female, but he wooed me for my
> thou in boundless confidence, until I graunted it. Hence I must
> slay him too, and sent him to his death by force and order.
> (501/VI 664)

Unlike his most illustrious literary progenitor, Goethe's Faust, Adrian cannot call into play a linguistic subterfuge in order to dupe his foe — Faust's use of the hypothetical subjunctive when speaking with the eager Mephistopheles: "Then to that moment I could say: Linger on...."[22] Leverkühn's satanic adversary had issued a blanket injunction against any and all love that "warms," and neither Adrian's recourse to the erotic in its homosexual modality (love for the non-feminine) nor a-sexual mode (adoration of the childlike, the other-worldly) proved to merit an exemption. His violation of the terms of the agreement incurred the most severe penalties: death in a form which, in the first instance, was demeaning, and, in the latter, dehumanizing.

Echo's angelic quality expresses itself in his appearance and his demeanor. Reading a picture book which his doting uncle has given him, the boy turns the pages of the text as would "the little angels up above ... their heavenly choir-books" (464/VI 616). However, having once descended from the celestial heights, it becomes inevitable that the cherubic boy forsake the music of the spheres and be drawn into the web of its more mundane counterpart. This comes about first of all through a harmless gift from Serenus, a music box,

---

[22]Johann Wolfgang von Goethe, *Faust*, Part One & Part Two, trans. Charles E. Passage (Indianapolis: Bobbs-Merrill, 1965), 393, ll. 11580-82.

which, nevertheless, sets in motion the process of the dis-integration of the ethereal and the integration of Nepo into the all too terrestrial: "three well-harmonized, demure little tinkling melodies, to which Echo listened always with the same rapt attention, the same unforgettable mixture of delight, surprise, and dreamy musing" (469/VI 623). Having been triggered by such innocuous and unpretentious stimuli, the musical virus, like its syphilitic counterpart in Adrian, begins an osmotic journey to the higher regions of the cerebrum.

Those same blue eyes which betrayed amusement at the demure, Biedermeier melodies of the music box soon gain access to music of the highest "order," compositions which owe their origins to darker, more demonic sources: "His uncle's manuscripts too, those runes strewn over the staves, adorned with little stems and tails, connected by slurs and strokes, some blank, some filled with black ..." (469/VI 623). As a member of that elitist group (which included Jeanette Scheurl, Rudi, and Frau Schweigestill) with whom Adrian is seen sitting or standing "hand-in-hand" (467/VI 620), Echo also shares something in common with Leverkühn's various erotic partners. He becomes intimately involved with the process of composition, as had been the case with Hetæra, von Tolna, and Schwerdtfeger — but significantly, not Marie Godeau.

> he [Echo] liked to look at them [Adrian's scores] too and have it explained what all those marks were about — just between ourselves, they were about him.... This child, sooner than any of us, was privileged to get an 'insight' into the drafts of the score of Ariel's songs, on which Adrian was privately at work. (469-70/VI 623)

Nepo, indeed, plays Ariel to Adrian's Prospero; the latter name, incidentally, derived from the Latin "prosperus," is a synonym for the other Latin word meaning "fortunate" or "lucky," namely "faustus."[23] The musical transcription succeeds through its "gossamer, whispering web" and "hovering childlike-pure, bewildering light swiftness" (470/VI 624) to capture in a tonal idiom of almost Mendelssohnian *Sommernachtstraum* quality, the idealized affection of the composer for this ethereal sprite.

In the characterization of Adrian as Prospero, the "good master of spells" (470/VI 624) from Shakespeare's *Tempest* who overcomes the wicked witch Sycorax, we have another instance of the "g" word allied with positive forces ("goodness"). A plethora of such concepts naturally surrounds the boy

---

[23]*Cassell's Latin Dictionary*, ed. D.P. Simpson (London: Cassell & Co., 1977), 242 and 483.

with the heavenly blue eyes, especially on those occasions when Adrian, due to headaches, has been shut away "in silence and darkness" (470/VI 624). Echo's bedtime prayers, punctuated with delightful mispronunciations or charming dialectical peculiarities such as "Godde" for "God" ("daß er 'Gott' immer wie 'Got' aussprach" [VI 625]), contain a plethora of such sounds: "Swelch Mensche lebt in Gotes Gebote,/ In dem ist Got und er in Gote" "Swie groß si jemands Missetat,/ Got dennoch mehr Genaden hat"; "Got lächelt in Seiner Gnadenfüll'"; "Guttat," etc. (VI 625). In a sense, Echo echoes in the lilt of his language the resonance of divine redemption; but the upshot of this appeal for God's grace through goodness is anything but propitious for Prospero. The sounds of Nepo's charming words as well as those of Ariel's music are all too soon drowned out by the child's screams of agony as the ravages of cerebrospinal meningitis produce head pains far outstripping the worst migraines of Adrian.

Medical science proves as inept when confronted with this fatal malady as it had been in the case of Adrian's incipient venereal disease; it can only offer makeshift remedies and stopgap measures. The pain is intensified for the reader's sensibilities by variations on a relentless ostinato refrain: "the frantic headache," "the skull-splitting headache," the "hydrocephalic shriek," the "shrieking, writhing torture" (475/VI 629-30). Finally, a merciful coma sets in and Nepomuk Schneidewein, Echo, the angelic child, Adrian's "last love," the lad who, up to this point, has been metaphorically or symbolically incorporated into Leverkühn's music (unlike Hetæra who is "literally" embodied in it) succumbs. The Faustian gambit, the linguistic sleight of hand fails; Prospero's gamble to outwit the forces of evil on semantic grounds by loving what was neither female nor "of this world" does not enjoy the prosperity of Goethe's "faustus."

At least this is so in the short run; in the long run, however, the results may be different. Adrian, in one of his rambling diatribes in the wake of Echo's passing, envisions a Faustian victory of the spirit of the law over the letter, and he hurls the following challenge to his hated foe, admonishing him in a hallucinatory moment:

> "Take his body, you have power over that. But you'll have to put up with leaving me his soul, his sweet and precious soul, that is where you lose out and make yourself a laughing-stock — and for that I will laugh you to scorn, æons on end. Let there be eternities rolled between my place and his, yet I shall know that he is there whence you were thrown out, orts and draff that you are!" (477/VI 632-33)

Of course, Adrian's unvarnished broadside is two-pronged. By "my place and his" he is undoubtedly referring to hell and heaven respectively. But the "place," in which Echo and Adrian's love for him have transcended death, is located in those "gossamer" compositions to Ariel, a "place" to which the adversary will never gain access. Here there is a secure niche in all eternity for the lad who was too perfect to endure life in the flawed fashion in which mere mortals must experience it.

As indicated earlier, however, there are several hints placed strategically throughout the account of Nepo-Echo which lead one to conjecture whether the "Gotteskindlein" may have had other dimensions to his make-up which betray traces of a somewhat less than divine origin. For instance, his smile which captivated the onlooker, was "not quite free from coquetry and consciousness of the charm he wielded" (461-62/VI 611). When a child *knows* that it is his childlikeness which fascinates adults, that child has already forfeited the quality of the childlike. The charming manikin actually issues a warning of dangers in the verses he recites: "A swordfish, a sawfish and shark" (466/VI 618). The inference is that such life-threatening forces can lurk unseen beneath the placid surface of the water. But could this also imply that under the veneer of an angelic little tyke there also lie forces threatening the well-being of those who come into contact with him? The azure of Nepo's sparkling eyes regard Serenus' well-meaning pedagogic tactics with "ironic understanding" (466/VI 618), suggesting a precociousness well beyond the boy's chronological years: "that elfin mockery seemed to express a consciousness of it" (466/VI 618-19). If Echo is intended to be the embodiment of the pure and perfect child, then his awareness of these traits in himself tends to subvert the very quality of childlike innocence they are meant to convey.

Once the meningitis has taken its course, Echo's agony, aside from the unbearable head-pains, is punctuated by his shrieks and "gnashing of teeth" (475, 476/VI 630, 635). This latter concept serves as a vivid reminder of the words of the adversary in Italy when he spoke, albeit evasively, of the plight of the denizens of Hell as being signaled by "wailing and gnashing of teeth" (245/VI 327). Gone from Echo are his "heaven's-blue eyes" (474/VI 630), and there remains only the "gnashing of teeth," not at all characteristic of a "child of God" but very endemic to the children of Hell.

Certainly what befalls Echo, whether the lad is intended to embody the good exclusively, the good permeated with elements of evil, or a state of being "beyond good and evil," makes his heart-rending lamentation ("herzzerreißendes Lamentieren" VI 630) the most drastic and devastating instance of the confluence of Eros-Melos-Thanatos in the novel. One might expect that, as a result of this harrowing experience, Adrian would retreat into stunned silence. He had done so for a year or more in the wake of Rudi's tragic death. Yet such is not the case after Nepo's terrible demise. The magnitude of the injustice seems to summon up in the composer a final musical response, one as radical in its conception as had been the inconceivable fate of the angelic Echo.

This work, the *Dr. Fausti Weheklag*, represents the apex of the strict style and summarizes Leverkühn's career, without, however, providing pat answers to the question: why did this all have to happen? Following his personal tragedies, Adrian creates the *Lamentation*, a consummate thematic statement of his life and the consummation of his technical skills as a composer. It is an open-ended work, which comes to a close but does not, by any means, achieve closure. And of course, it not only pays homage to Echo in a musically encoded manner, but it also brings the symbolic "g" tone to what may be regarded as either a turning point or a point of no return.

Already in his *Apocalypsis cum figuris* of 1919 we had been confronted with the horrors of hell as presented by Dante's words from the *Inferno* and re-presented by Dürer's woodcuts. But in close proximity to the scene of terrible perdition in the former work, "Grace [personified in the German text as "die Gnade"] draws up two sinning souls from the snare into redemption" (358/VI 476). Thus in this oratorio, which in its unrelenting pessimism, serves as a precursor to the *Lamentation* of 1928-1930, a key concept for salvation is conveyed by a word beginning with "g." The potential for redemption through one's own good deeds or through God's grace stands in close proximity — if not reciprocity — to sin and destruction. Of course, it is not stated *expressis verbis* that the allegorical figure of Gnade in its musical setting is to be linked to the note "g." By the same token, at the conclusion of Leverkühn's *Lamentation*, when all instrumental groups have left the stage one by one, only a single cello remains sounding the ethereal "high G ... the last word, the last fainting sound, slowly dying in a pianissimo-fermata" (491/VI 651). On this occasion, with only the symbolically significant note "g" lingering on, nothing is said *expressis verbis* about grace, goodness, or God. But since so much suggestive of these entities has been introduced throughout the preceding 650 pages of the novel, one is tempted to associate the musical tone with such phonetic counterparts in the verbal medium.

Serenus himself describes the finale of this last musical work and, as usual, interjects a personal perspective into what he reports — especially regarding the silence that comes in the wake of the final "g:"

> Then nothing more: silence, and night. But that tone which vibrates in the silence, which is no longer there, to which only the spirit hearkens, and which was the voice of mourning, is no

more. It changes its meaning; it abides as a light in the night. (491/VI 651)

The spiritual tone, no longer acoustically perceptible but "audible" to the spirit alone, had been a melancholy sound, a part of the general lamentation. But by some miracle which transcends the intellect but not belief, the meaning of the isolated, orphan sound changes — one almost might say in terms of a pun in English, from "mourning" to "morning." This linguistic by-play may seem superficial, but it has a function in probing the deep-structure of the novel.

Shortly after his return from Pressburg and Hetæra (1906), Adrian had taken Dante passages from *Purgatorio* and *Paradiso* "chosen with a shrewd sense of their affinity with music" (162/VI 215) as texts for songs. These included verses "where the poet in the light of the planet Venus sees the smaller lights — they are the spirits of the blessed — some more quickly, the others more slowly, 'according to the kind of their regard of God,' drawing their circles ..." (162/VI 215). Recalling that Venus is not only the name of the goddess of love, but also a designation for the planet which, as the morning star, is also referred to as Lucifer, then the relevance of this early passage to the *Lamentation* becomes clearer, as does the preponderance of "g" concepts. This letter symbolism not only applies to the positive elements in these songs ("Gesänge") such as "Geister der Seligen," and "Gottbetrach-tung" (VI 215), but also to concepts which convey positive values, if only by negating the negative: "Gottes Tiefe," "Gerechtigkeit ..., die den Guten und Reinen, nur eben nicht Getauften, vom Glauben nicht Erreichten," "die Ohnmacht des geschöpflich Guten vor dem Guten an sich" (162/VI 216).

Adrian's existential status encompasses both the "bad" light of Venus-Lucifer and the good, but "smaller lights" as the "spirit of the blessed" circling in their orbits around God. The positive Dante songs of "light in light" (162/VI 216) are contrasted with those of the same poet which are more introspective (the "morning-mourning" dichotomy cited above), where there is a "questioning, wrestling with the unfathomable" and where doubt reigns for "even the cherub who looks into God's depths" (162/VI 216). Here is the other side of the coin, the same kind of "questioning" which, at the close of the *Lamentation*, still remains unanswered as the final "g" fades from earshot, only to persist synaesthetically as "light in the night."

Before examining this oratorio in detail, a final link to the Dante songs should be mentioned. In conjunction with the latter, Serenus had admired the "moving musical diction" ascribed to the parable from the *Purgatorio* of the "man who carries a light on his back at night, which does not light him but lights up the path of those coming after" (163/VI 217). The allegorical poem itself speaks so "darkly and difficultly" (163/VI 217) that Serenus sees no prospect of its hidden sense being understood by the world. Instead of trying to fathom its meaning, the reader should simply appreciate its beauty: "The way the music strives upward out of the difficulties, the artful confusion, the mingled distresses of its first part to the tender light of the final cry and there is touchingly resolved ..." (163/VI 217). We have here in these Dante settings a precursor of the *Lamentation*, the last work of a man who may, indeed, have passed from "deep night into the deepest night of all" (3/VI 9), as the very first page of the novel informs us. But is there perhaps a glimmer of hope that Adrian resembled that man from Dante's fable who carried a light on his back to illuminate the way for those who came behind him, to "enlighten" them by his career as man and artist? Could that be another echelon of meaning to that otherwise unfathomable "g" which abides as a light in the night, as his musical legacy to posterity? A closer look at the *Lamentation* may help clarify this issue or, conversely, lead to the conclusion that this ambiguity, like so many other ambivalencies in the novel, best remains "the unanswered question."

Conceived originally in 1927, even before Nepo-Echo's horrible death, the *Lamentation of Dr. Faustus* was only completed and put to paper at the time when "the tormenting attacks of headache" (483/VI 641) had temporarily abated. But the ravages of this disease had gradually begun to leave their permanent mark: Adrian, his head tilted to one side, now appears spiritualized, almost Christlike in an "ecce-homo" pose. The physical deterioration had been accompanied by the anguish of his personal martyrdom: the shipwreck of his marriage plans, the loss of his only true friend, and the snatching away of the marvelous child. Finally, the musical stage had been set by Jeanette Scheurl, that paragon of caritative love and devotion, who supplied the anchorite Adrian with some seventeenth-century music. This included the aforementioned baroque chaconne which anticipated unspecified passages from *Tristan und Isolde*. Leverkühn's interest in the early Baroque period had been previously restricted to the music of Monteverdi. It is now these two ostensibly incompatible works and worlds, the seventeenth century and the nineteenth, the age responsible for establishing the diatonic harmony and the period in which that fundamental tonality began to falter, that join forces.

The task of deliberately "taking back" or negating the "joy" of Beethoven's setting of Schiller's ode "An die Freude" in his symphonic testament begins with an allusion to the biblical lament of the forlorn servant in the wilderness crying out "de profundis." In keeping with the close Brentano ties in Leverkühn's work and the fact that the initial composition in his repertoire utilizing the "strict style" was the cycle of thirteen songs based on lyrics by that poet, one might cite in this context Brentano's poem of 1816, "Frühlingsschrei eines Knechtes aus der Tiefe." Following his "de profundis" observation, Serenus draws our attention to the *"lasciatemi morire"* of Ariadne, a mournful aria echoed by a chorus of nymphs (486/VI 644). Zeitblom does not identify his source at this point, but the reference is most likely to the famous "Lamento," the only extant fragment of Monteverdi's opera *L'Arianna* of 1608. On the other hand, this allusion might also find reverberations in the Strauß-Hofmannsthal *Ariadne auf Naxos* of 1912. For the final time, an opera title becomes a cipher-symbol in the novel for an entire complex of meanings and motifs. Even the femine form of the name, Ariadne, could be regarded as a scrambled anagram for Adrian, with the final vowel "e" a necessary addendum for the gender change. In the myth, Ariadne is forsaken by her lover and left on the isle of Naxos, where she is awakened and wooed by Dionysos, whom she considers an emissary of death. The incorporation of this mythical tale as prime substance indicates that to the very end Eros and Thanatos stand under the aegis of Melos.

Very early in his musical studies in Leipzig with Kretzschmar and shortly after the fateful sojourn in Pressburg-Graz (1906), Adrian and his mentor had taken a journey to Basel where they heard a number of seventeenth-century works performed, with Monteverdi's *Magnificat* being featured. Adrian characterized this composition as an "outburst of modernity in Monteverdi's musical devices" (177/VI 237), because such "musica riservata" exhibited emotion and expressiveness which "is a rebound from the constructivism of the Netherlanders" (177/VI 237). Finally, this music is said to have made a "strong and lasting" impression on Adrian. This was certainly the case, for both the *Apocalypsis* and the *Lamentation* present clear-cut evidence of constructivism paired with expressivity.

A further, more personalized dimension of relevance to Adrian's career in the *Lamentation* is articulated by Serenus in another of his remarks which, in spite of its perceptiveness, proves to be remarkably imperceptive:

> It does not lack significance that the *Faust* cantata is stylistically so strongly and unmistakably linked with the seventeenth century and Monteverdi, whose music — again not without significance — favored the echo-effect, sometimes to the point of being a mannerism. The echo, the giving back of the human voice as nature-sound, and the revelation of it *as* nature-sound, is essentially a lament: ... In Leverkühn's last and loftiest creation, echo, favorite device of the baroque, is employed with unspeakably mournful effect. (486/VI 644)

Can Serenus be so short-sighted as not to draw the obvious inference from the predominance of the echo-effect in this work of lamentation? Was not the most resounding "echo" in Adrian's entire lifetime Nepomuk Schneidewein? Is it not the latter's fate which is now being "echoed" before our very ears? Yet neither here nor later, when reiterating his observations on the antiphonal device, does it occur to Serenus even to mention the name of the angelic lad. Does Serenus commit another of his blunders of judgment, this time failing to see the implicit message of the music in his zeal to properly identify the medium of that message?

The principle of *coincidentia oppositorum* had been extrinsically in operation in the "dear-evil" text of the Brentano song as well as that of the holy sinner Gregory, and intrinsically in force in the music of the *Apocalypsis*.[24] Thus we heard in conjunction with the latter that there obtained "the substantial identity of the most blest with the most accurst, the inner unity of the chorus of child angels and the hellish laughter of the damned" (486/VI 645). Much in the same manner as in those earlier Dante songs, where the proximity — and contiguity — of good and evil had been stressed ("Venus-gestirn" [Lucifer] — "Gottbetrachtung," VI 215), so now in the *Lamentation* the reciprocity of the conflicting forces is underscored. The lamentations move out in ever-widening concentric circles (487/VI 645), like ringlets of water radiating from the point where a stone has been tossed into a pond. This centrifugal movement is reminiscent of the orbiting lights in the Dante songs "drawing their circles" according to the nature "of their regard of God" (162/VI 215).

The waves radiating in circular fashion are likened to the myriad variations of a central theme in the chapters of a literary work which, as it turns out, is then identified as the venerable chapbook of Dr. Faustus (1587). The passage alluded to from this source is the famous farewell confession of the necromancer to his assembled guests: "'For I die as a good and as a bad Christian'" (487); "'Denn ich sterbe als ein böser und guter Christ'" (VI 646). This forms the core of Adrian's monumental set of lamentations, which takes back the "ode to joy" just as the *Gesta* nullified the lofty word-tone conceptions of Wagnerian stamp.

As had been the case with the *Apocalypsis*, where the "profoundest mystery of this music" was "the mystery of identity" (378/VI 502), one can observe in Leverkühn's neo-Monteverdian lamentation the same principle in operation with regard to the variation of the fundamental Dr. Faustus paradox. Thematic substance and musical technique now coincide in their modus operandi: the "bad-good" dichotomy forms

---

[24]For the most recent and thoroughgoing treatment of this aspect of the legend and of Mann's novel, see Alfred Hoelzel, *The Paradoxical Quest: A Study of Faustian Vicissitudes*, New Yorker Beiträge zur Vergleichenden Literaturwissenschaft, Bd. 1 (New York: Lang, 1988), especially 117-58.

> ... the basis of all the music — or rather, it lies almost as key behind everything and is responsible for the identity of the most varied forms — that identity which exists between the crystalline angelic choir and the hellish yelling in the *Apocalypse* and which has now become all-embracing: a formal treatment strict to the last degree, which no longer knows anything unthematic, in which the order of the basic material becomes total ... there is no longer any free note. (487-88/VI 646)

Seen from this perspective, even Dr. Faustus' evocation of Helena from the realm of the shades becomes an "echo" and variation of Orpheus' rescue mission of Eurydice (the archetypal Melos-Eros-Thanatos myth) from the underworld. Can such lofty feats of the past have their counterpart in Adrian's own descent to the underworld of Hetæra Esmeralda and his ascent with her to the heights of modern musical creativity?

In spite of Serenus' elaborate analysis of the central oxymoron and his doting on the echo-principle manifest in the variations, the narrator still fails to link either of these with Echo himself. Not only does the "heart-rending lamentation" (475/VI 630) of the dying boy "echo" in this musical testament; evident, too, is his divine appearance obfuscated by its diabolic aftermath. The adversary in Italy had refused to articulate what the "wailing and gnashing of teeth" characteristic of the inhabitants of Hell would be like, since words, the verbal icon, were not adequate to describe this din (244/VI 326-27). Yet even though "clumsy words" and the "inadequacy of language to arrive at visualization or to produce an exact portrait" of Echo (462/VI 612) prevent Serenus from satisfactorily describing the angelic beauty of the boy, they do appropriately render his agony: his "shrieking" and "gnashing of the teeth" (475/VI 630). The juxtaposition of a heavenly face and a hellish fate in the same boy, however, gives one grounds to suspect a *coincidentia oppositorum* condition even where it would be least likely expected.

In keeping with what the narrator pinpoints as a "sense of résumé" (488/VI 647) in the *Weheklag*, a recapitulation constituting a kind of "echo" in itself, he underscores the appearance of the five-note Hetæra Esmeralda figure, which, according to him, had permeated Adrian's entire creative output subsequent to its initial articulation. Only on this final occasion does Serenus actually specify what the significance of the motif is: "in *Faustus* too that letter symbol, the Hetæra-Esmeralda figure, first perceived by me, very often governs melody and harmony: that is to say, everywhere where there is reference to the bond and the vow, the promise and the blood pact" (489/VI 648).

But with regard to the manner or method of musical integration Serenus remains tight-lipped, perhaps tongue-tied would be a more suitable term. By the same token, he fails to offer any detailed explanation of exactly how the twelve syllables of the Faustian lament were to be set to music. He simply states that in the *Lamentation* there is a principal theme, "the kernel of which, out of which everything develops, is just that twelve-note idea" (489/VI 648). We know from previous theoretical discussions, however, that Adrian early on perceived the limitations of the five-note Hetæra motif. He stated already at that time (1910), that this system of transfer from letter or syllables to musical coefficients would have to be expanded to include all twelve tones from the tempered scale. But the text supplies not a single clue as to how this is accomplished in the *Weheklag*. This remains a perplexing "unanswered question."

However, it is significant that once the Faustian "bad-good" variations and the Hetærean "dear-evil" theme have run their course in Adrian's musical swan song, the vocal segments of the oratorio conclude. It is left to the orchestral voices alone, to "tones without words," to make the ultimate statement. Instrumental music, devoid of the semantic ties stemming from a literary text, is allowed to speak with that "speaking unspokenness given to music alone" (490/VI 650). Just as the hallmark of the entire *Lamentation* — as well as of Adrian's post-1906 compositions in the new idiom — had been the conjunction of seemingly disjunctive or even antinomic entities, so we have another variation of such paradoxes: the articulate inarticulateness of music. Such may be the proper aesthetic medium in which to pose the dilemma of all dilemmas: how a renewed sense of emotion or feeling, "bovine warmth," if you will, can emanate from the most mathematically precise, coldly calculated constructivist art.

But it is not enough that the chorus cedes precedence to the orchestra at the close of this work; even the latter undergoes a reduction to minimalist proportions insofar as only a single instrument — a cello — is heard at the end, sounding a single note, the often mentioned "g." Three aspects of this situation deserve consideration. First of all, the instrument in question is of the non-tempered variety, a member of the string family which can produce true tones in all their purity, as opposed to the tempered group (such as the piano). The latter made possible much of the enharmonic interchange which led to music's essential "ambiguity" ("Zweideutigkeit") coming to the fore in the post-Bachian period. On this occasion, however, such ambivalence is superseded by pristine tones which should preclude all equivocation. Secondly, the progression to be observed in Adrian Leverkühn's musical career has been from parodistic imitation of the old to innovation of the new, from contrapuntal canons, polyphony, and harmony to "crab" canons, their retrograde counterparts, atonality, and dodecaphony. Given the nature of this enigmatic ending on an isolated "g," however, we almost have a turning back to the most primitive form of music, to monody, and this development comes in the wake of the most complex evolution of the art possible. A return to fundamentals, to the "fundamental" in the sense of "re-ligio," perhaps, if we regard "g" — as has been the case up to now — as the letter symbol for God; God, who through His Grace and the sinful individual's inherent goodness, becomes reconciled with the sinner in a kind of theodicean interrelationship. And if God's love as Caritas represents the ultimate modality of Eros, could one perhaps not also conjecture that the particular twelve-tone row, which Adrian devises to accommodate Faustus as both a "bad" and a "good" Christian and which culminates on "g," is likewise imbued with such sublime symbolic potential?[25]

Proceeding then, to Serenus' closing remarks on the *Weheklag*, that after even the "g" has become acoustically inaudible, it may still vibrate in the silence and darkness which follows as "light in the night," one may regard this merely as a case of wishful thinking or listening. However, is it not feasible that, in a universe in which "relationship is everything," sound, too, might become perceptible in another modality? The aural transmutes into the visual, a synaesthetic transference of the kind so favored by writers in the romantic era. The "light" in question, stems from that "g" of the cello, which is the note "sol" in the scale of "C," that basic key in which divine Caritas seems to find its most powerful symbolic expression. The word "sol" of course, is the Latin term for "sun" (as in solar), and so it may not be too far-fetched to speculate that a "faustus," a "prosperus" individual, is the one who can, in the final reckoning, pay homage to a beneficent love from above in the form of "[sun]light in the night."

Even the concept of night can be interpreted in terms of the Melos-Eros-Thanatos triad, since, as previously indicated, the very first page of the novel alludes to Adrian's death as his having passed from "deep night into the deepest night of all." From the musical standpoint, however, this is a transition not into the realm of unmitigated darkness, but rather to one which exudes a

---

[25]In a lecture delivered at the "Thomas Mann Symposium: *Doctor Faustus* at the Margin of Modernism," held at the University of California, Irvine in March, 1988, I sought to summarize the thesis of the present study by outlining twelve modalities of love ranging from the "bad" to the "good" and their role in Leverkühn's life and work. The talk, entitled "Melos, Eros, Thanatos and *Doctor Faustus*" received mixed reactions, due basically to an expected Freudian interpretation of the Eros-Thanatos components which I, however, did not intend to present. The title, of course, pointed in this direction, and the respondent at the symposium, Martin Schwab, justifiably criticized this shortcoming.

radiance of its own — akin to that propagated by the Romantics a century and a half earlier.[26]

As Leverkühn prepares to play a piano rendition of his *Weheklag* for a hand-picked audience at the Schweigestills in Pfeiffering after a public confession of his transgressions, he attacks the keys of the brown square piano "in a strongly dissonant chord" (503/VI 667). This raises several interesting possibilities. I have argued elsewhere that it might be possible to correlate the twelve syllables of the confession about dying as a bad and a good Christian with the twelve tones of the scale as well as with twelve modalities of love — good as well as bad — found in the novel (from the maternal "chaste reserve" to divine Caritas).[27] Were this to be the case, could the "strongly dissonant chord" at the opening of Leverkühn's musical legacy be suggestive of something more than a mere random conglomeration of cacophonous sound? After all, the final movement of Beethoven's Ninth — the work which Adrian seeks to negate — also opens with a startling dissonance. Could Adrian's dissonant chord possibly consist of the twelve tones in his row for the Faustus' confession, simply sounded simultaneously rather than in sequence? While still a pupil of Kretzschmar, Adrian had been fascinated by the teacher's theories of how linear melody could be converted to vertical harmony, and in essence a similar principle is functioning here.

Adrian's closing comments just before striking this initial chord make liberal use of the "g" consonant: he alludes to "good — grace — God" as "gut — Gnade — Gott" (VI 666) and then, in variant form: "for my good ... Grace and forgiveness ... Everlasting Goodness." For this the German has "mir ... zugute gehalten ... Gnade und Verzeihung ... die ewige Güte" (VI 666). Immediately prior to his final collapse there comes a plea "hold me in kindly remembrance ..." ("ihr wollt meiner im Guten gedenken" [503/VI 666]). Even while confessing that the source of his musical transgression can be ascribed only to the Devil, Leverkühn does so in an acoustically provocative manner: he claims to be playing "from the construction which I heard from the lovely instrument of Satan" — "aus dem Gefüge spielen, das ich dem lieblichen Instrument des Satans abgehört" (530/VI 666). The word "Gefüge" is, like the "Tonsetzer" in the title of the novel, a somewhat unusual and far from

---

[26]The essay cited in footnote 25 also deals peripherally with the Romanic roots and sources of such synaesthetic concepts as the light of the night.

[27]The lecture at the Irvine Thomas Mann symposium outlined twelve modalities of love in the work ranging from the crassly sensual to the sublime Caritas and these twelve varieties of love, so the argument went, were then transferred to the serial row in his *Lamentation*, thus constituting the core of the work.

commonplace term for a musical composition, and as such commands special attention. Through its phonemic components alone it alerts the reader to the fact that music has been the source of the damnation of Faust(us) as well as of his salvation. The "-füge" portion with its stress on construction, on the fitting together of parts, is, phonically speaking, a distant cousin several times removed of the "Fuge" of the "O homo fuge" family. Adrian failed to heed the warning implied in the Latin and opted instead for the musical interpretation: rather than flee music, he took flight to the fugue, with all the Icarian consequences thereof. The "Ge—" prefix, on the other hand, belongs to the cluster of "g" sounds which dominate in verbal concepts denoting qualities of divine love or avenues leading to reconciliation with the Godhead.

Adrian's plea that his memory be kept favorably ("im Guten") becomes transposed to yet another key following his complete collapse at the piano. Mrs. Schweigestill, his surrogate mother in Pfeiffering and the practitioner of caritative love, tends the now fallen Icarus and proclaims in her inimitable Bavarian dialect: "Viel hat er von der ewigen Gnaden g'redt" (VI 667). Her statement contains a triad of "g's" in close proximity ("— gen Gnaden g'redt"), and her south-German patois could be as cryptic for some to fathom as was the esoteric nature of the "g" in the high register of the cello in Adrian's closing musical statement.

With the *Weheklag* Adrian Leverkühn's music grows silent, his affiliations with love have long ago run their course, and only death waits in the wings for its appointed hour. The novel, too, has come to a close, offering no solution or resolution, but merely leaving most problems unresolved. For instance, the ties of Leverkühn to the fate of Germany remain cloudy. The thorny issue of the "German question" — perhaps crystallized most vividly in the coexistence within the radius of Weimar of monuments to German culture and the crematoria of Buchenwald within a few kilometers of each other — remain unanswered — a "final solution" to which the world will perhaps never find the solution. Cold calculation and intense emotional fervor coinciding geographically in Weimar, worked hand in hand on the politico-racial level just as they had done on the aesthetic plane in Leverkühn's music. In fact, despite the many instances cited by our unreliable narrator in his myriad variations of the "mystery of identity," the *coincidentia oppositorum* remains just that at the end: a mystery. Serenus is never able to explain satisfactorily exactly how angelic choirs and the hellish host share common musical means in the *Apocalypsis* — he simply asserts that they do. We were not told how the dear-evil oxymoron could be transcribed musically neither within the confines of the five-note Hetæra Esmeralda motif nor in the larger expanse of the good-bad Christian configuration. Because such fundamental existential as well as musical queries remain in limbo, it might perhaps be fitting to conclude by casting another glance at the point of departure for this study: Leonard Bernstein's Harvard Lectures published as *The Unanswered Question.*

The title for this series of talks (directed to the knowledgeable layman rather than the musical expert), was taken from a composition originally written in 1906 by the American composer Charles Ives: "The Unanswered Question." This year proved to be a crucial temporal axis for artistic ferment on the cusp of modernity. It coincided, chronologically, with the fictional portrayal of Leverkühn's "breakthrough" to Eros, with his evolution of a radically innovative technique of musical composition (Melos), and with the venereal infection which both sparked this creative surge and yet paved the way for his death (Thanatos). Ives, like Leverkühn, was an avant-garde artist almost half a century before his time.[28] Even though Ives' idiosyncratic symphonies and orchestral pieces had to wait until the 1950s and 1960s to gain a place in the "canon," they were already being performed in the late 1940s. Since this is the time when Mann was completing *Doctor Faustus*, it is tempting to speculate whether he might have ever heard any of them played on the Sunday afternoon radio broadcasts of the New York Philharmonic. Other possible avenues of access to Ives' works might have been Mann's musical mentor, Theodor Adorno, or possibly his youngest son, Michael Mann, an accomplished musician whose own offspring, Frido, served as a model for Nepo-Echo.

Ives wrote the following description for "The Unanswered Question" and, in spite of obvious differences between his composition and the close of the *Weheklag* some significant parallels and analogies can be drawn:

[28]Vivian Perlis in *Charles Ives Remembered* (New Haven: Yale University Press, 1974), 144-45, recalls a performance of "The Unanswered Question" on May 11, 1946, for the Ditson Festival at Columbia University. But since Mann was living in Pacific Palisades, California, during this year and came to New York in 1947 only for a lecture, it is not likely that he ever heard any of Ives' music played there (the New York Philharmonic began to feature Ives' works prominently only after Leonard Bernstein introduced the Second Symphony in 1951).

According to one biographer of Ives, David Wooldridge, *From the Steeples and Mountains. A Study of Charles Ives* (New York: Knopf, 1974), 282, however, the composer did not think highly of serial music. Wooldridge notes, 282: "he [Ives] implied later, in response to the French critic who thought he must have been influenced by Schoenberg that he didn't think much of Schoenberg either. Yet he continually felt drawn. 'The Devil tempted me. . . .' — Faust's problem. Perhaps this is another reason why Ives stopped composing, because he saw serial writing as the only musical avenue left, and his few expeditions into that territory frightened him. Thomas Mann's *Doktor Faustus* was a 12-tone composer. Maybe Ives saw himself like Faust — like Ahab — having to make a compact with the Devil, signed in his own blood. . . ."

The strings play *ppp* [pianississimo] throughout with no change in tempo. They are to represent "The Silences of the Druids — who Know, See and Hear Nothing." The trumpet intones "The Perennial Question of Existence" and states it in the same tone of voice each time. But the hunt for "The Invisible Answer" undertaken by the flutes and other human beings becomes gradually more active, faster and louder.... "The Fighting Answers," as the time goes on, ... seem to realize a futility and begin to mock "The Question" — the strife is over for the moment. After they disappear, "The Question" is asked for the last time, and the "Silences" are heard beyond in "Undisturbed Solitude."[29]

The perennial, but unanswered question of existence is posed by a recurrent trumpet theme consisting of a five-note motif (shades of Hetæra Esmeralda's ubiquitous musical signature). It is sounded in ostinato fashion and in clashing atonality with the pianissimo strings throughout the short piece (the duration of which is about six minutes).[30] There is a gradual reduction in dynamic range, so that at the close only the timbre of a single instrumental family

---

[29]*Charles E. Ives, The Unanswered Question for Trumpet, Flute Quartet, and Strings*, critical edition, ed. Paul C. Echols and Noel Zahler (New York: Peer, 1984), "Score," 10.

[30]Ives, *The Unanswered Question*, pages 2 and 9, 11 and 19 of the "Score," show the opening and closing measures of the 1906 and 1930 versions respectively. They reveal that the composition in its original and later adaptation begins and ends with the strings ("con scordini") in "G." The final has the first violins sustaining a high "g" moving from the "ppp" to "pppp," while the celli intone the same note four octaves lower. The five-note, atonal trumpet theme, although repeated seven times in both versions, undergoes an interesting metamorphosis in the later scoring:

1906:

1930 the form in the first, third, fifth and seventh appearance:

1930 on alternate or even occasions, the contour changes as follows:

124

persists: "The strings will continue their last chord for two measures or so after the trumpet stops." The composer's description of the "silences" which seem to resonate ever so slightly and envelop these ethereal sounds only to be "heard beyond in 'Undisturbed Solitude' " — is very reminiscent of Serenus' account of the final moments of the *Weheklag*.

But most striking when one compares the two works is the fact that both modern composers, factual and fictional, select the "G" tonality in which to make a seminal, but cryptic, closing musical statement. To be sure, Ives actually has an open fifth while Leverkühn calls for a single tone, the fundamental; and even though both score their finale for the strings alone, we are given no aesthetic guidelines or authorial guidance as to why the key of "G" was chosen. Throughout the latter part of this investigation, it has been suggested that in a novel, in which letter symbolism and musical notation are constantly correlated with one another, there might also be a hidden semantic connection between this note and verbal concepts denoting a sense of divine redemption or reconciliation. The composer Ives banishes the conflict between consonance and dissonance, sound and silence, questioning and answering, finality and eternity, and a host of other implied dichotomies, to the realm of ambiguity and ambivalence. This equivocal stance was akin to that "Zweideutigkeit," to which Adrian, early on in his musical dabblings — in fact, during his first serious encounter with the tonal art at the harmonium in his uncle's shop — had also relegated it: "Relation-ship is everything. And if you want to give it a more precise name, it is ambiguity...."

Serenus' very last words in the novel once again have recourse to the all-important "g" consonant and, indeed, deal with the concept of God's loving grace: "Gott sei euerer armen Seele gnädig, mein Freund, mein Vaterland" ("God be merciful to thy poor soul, my friend, my Fatherland" [510/VI 676]). The specter of narratological "wishful thinking" again looms large on the horizon. Can one in the same breath implore loving grace from a transcendent source for the man of music who risked death for the cause of modern art and for a nation which staked its welfare on a death-dealing political ideology? By means of the echo-effect of double alliteration in a triad of verbal-semantic ciphers and signifiers (**G**ott — **gn**ädig, **m**ein Freund, **m**ein Vaterland) Serenus, perhaps serendipitously, tries to cement a spiritual bond between the destiny of the German composer and the fate of the country of Germany.

Any investigation of *Doctor Faustus* which hopes to do justice to the novel's complexity and taunting evasiveness, however, would be well advised to abide by a kind of *caveat lector* principle when drawing wide-sweeping conclusions. In an age when "the center cannot hold,"[31] at a time, in fact, when we even seem to suffer from a "loss of center,"[32] it would be presumptive at best and foolhardy at worst to propose one-dimensional interpretations of Mann's multidimensional novel. Consequently, the Melos-Eros-Thanatos framework which, in the short run of this study, seemed to offer a set of heuristic variations giving some continuity to the elusive text, may, in the long run of critical scrutiny, prove chimeric. As such, it would be tantamount to the high "g" at the close of the *Weheklag* which Serenus, our not always reliable narrator when chronicling the rise and fall of Adrian Leverkühn in tandem with that of Germany during the twentieth century, *thinks* he hears in the silence and *believes* he sees as light in the night.

[31]William Butler Yeats, "The Second Coming," in: *The Norton Anthology of English Literature*, ed. M.H. Abrams et al., vol. 2 (New York: Norton, 1962) 1355.

[32]Sedlmayr, *Verlust der Mitte.*

Quotations in the Original German from Mann's 'Doktor Faustus'

Page references are to Volume VI of the *Gesammelte Werke in zwölf Bänden*:

9	aus tiefer Nacht in die tiefste gegangen....
13	Wen hätte dieser Mann geliebt? Einst eine Frau — vielleicht. Ein Kind zuletzt — es mag sein. Einen leichtwiegenden, jeden gewinnenden Fant und Mann aller Stunden, den er dann, wahrscheinlich eben weil er ihm geneigt war, von sich schickte — und zwar in den Tod.
23	in volltönendem Farbendreiklang
26	die passenden Gefäße für Gifte und Liebestränke
34	Neigung zur Migräne
35	einer Stallmagd namens Hanne, einer Person mit Schlotterbusen und nackten, ewig mistigen Füßen
41	mit der der kleine Adrian darum auf freundschaftlichem Fuße stand, weil sie zu singen liebte und mit uns Kindern kleine Gesangsübungen zu veranstalten pflegte.
41	einer Art von Keuschheit
41	damit ging dieses tierisch duftende Geschöpf höchst frei heraus und sang uns, zwar mit plärrender Stimme, aber gutem Gehör, ... allerlei Volks-, Soldaten- und auch Gassenlieder, meist gefühlstriefenden oder grausigen Charakters vor....
41	daß es auf dem Hofe ... , Adrians späterem Aufenthaltsort, gewiß nicht überraschenderweise, auch eine Stallmagd mit Waberbusen und ewig mistigen Barfüßen gab, die der Hanne von Buchel so ähnlich sah, wie eben eine Stallmagd der andern ähnlich sieht ...
41-42	Sangen wir dann mit, so fiel sie in die Terz, aus der sie, wie es sich traf, in die Unterquint und Untersext sprang, und überließ uns die Oberstimme, indem sie ostentativ und ohrenfällig die zweite behauptete.
42	Dabei pflegte sie, wahrscheinlich um uns zur rechten Würdigung des harmonischen Vergnügens aufzufordern, ganz ähnlich lachend das Gesicht in die Breite zu ziehen wie Suso....

schwörende Stück, das mit der unheimlich moralischen Warnung endigt: "Hüte dich! Sei wach und munter!"

106   immer zwielichtiges, vom Tode berührtes Genie

112   denn ist nicht der Augenblick des Flüggewerdens und anbrechender Freiheit, wenn das Tor der Schule sich hinter uns schließt, das Stadtgehäuse, in dem wir herangezogen worden, sich auftut und die Welt uns offen liegt, der glücklichste oder doch der erregend erwartungsvollste in unser aller Leben? Durch seine musikalischen Ausflüge mit Wendell Kretzschmar in größere Nachbarstädte hatte Adrian ein paarmal am weltlichen Draußen im voraus genippt... .

152   gerade auf das Klavier zuzugehen, als sei dieses das eigentliche Ziel seines Weges hierher gewesen ... als suche er Zuflucht dort

173   den Beruf zu wechseln und sich ganz der Musik in die Arme zu werfen

175   seit ich kein von Fach zu Fach springender Junggeselle mehr bin, sondern verheiratet mit einem Beruf, einem Studium, hat es sich zusammen mit ihr ins oft schon recht Arge verstärkt.

Großer Gott, Sie werden nicht glauben, daß ich mich für zu schade halte für jeden Beruf. Im Gegenteil: es ist mir schade um jeden, den ich zu dem meinen mache, und Sie mögen eine Huldigung für — eine Liebeserklärung an die Musik darin sehen, eine Ausnahmestellung zu ihr, daß es mir um sie ganz besonders schade wäre.

177   Diese Eigenschaft ... sei der Ausdruck des Mangels an Wärme, an Sympathie, an Liebe, — und es frage sich allzusehr, ob man mit ihr überhaupt zum Künstler, das heiße denn doch wohl immer: zum Liebhaber und zum Geliebten der Welt tauge.

178   (begleitet vom Hauptweh)

182   "Sie sind schon zwanzig, und Sie haben sich noch eine Menge knifflichen Handwerks anzueignen, schwierig genug, um Sie zu reizen. Es ist besser, von Kanon-, Fugen- und Kontrapunkt-Exerzitien Hauptweh zu bekommen als von der Widerlegung der Kant'schen Widerlegung der Gottesbeweise. Genug des theologischen Jungfernstandes!

Die Jungfrauschaft ist wert, doch muß sie Mutter werden,
Sonst ist sie wie ein Plan von unbefruchter Erden."

184   sich ganz der Musik in die Arme warf.

185   unser Kanon-Singen mit der Stall-Hanne unter der Linde.

188   einen ganzen Stapel schnurriger Canon- und Fugen- Studien

188   die mechanische Trennung von Kontrapunkt und Harmonie, sintemal sie einander so unlöslich durchdringen, daß man nicht jedes für sich, sondern nur das Ganze, nämlich Musik lehren kann, — sofern man es kann.

188   das Dominospiel mit den Akkorden

190   sehe mir gegenüber ein offen Klavier, einen Freund, geh über den Teppich drauf los und schlage im Stehen zwei, drei Akkorde an, weiß noch, was es war, weil mir das Klang-phänomen gerade im Sinne lag, Modulation von H- nach C-Dur, aufhellender Halbton-Abstand wie im Gebet der Eremiten im Freischütz-Finale, bei dem Eintritt von Pauke, Trompeten und Oboen auf dem Quartsextakkord von C.

191   eine Bräunliche

192   "Nimm das cis-Moll-Notturno opus 27 No.1 und den Zwiege-sang, der angeht nach der enharmonischen Vertauschung von Cis- mit Des-Dur. Das übertrifft an desperatem Wohlklang alle Tristan-Orgien — und zwar in klavieristischer Intimität, nicht als Hauptschlacht der Wollust und ohne das Corridahafte einer in der Verderbtheit robusten Theatermystik.

192   die sublime Inzucht seiner phantastisch delikaten und verführer-ischen Kunst

193   Facetie und Büffelposse

193   mit musikkritischen Aperçus

193   Alles übrige war Zutat, Einhüllung, Vorwand, Aufschub ...

194   "Lusthölle"

195   niemals anders als durch das Medium von Kunst und Literatur, anläßlich der Manifestationen der Leidenschaft in der Sphäre des Geistes, hatte dies Wesen in unseren Austausch hinein-gespielt, und dabei waren sachlich wissende Äußerungen von seiner Seite gefallen, bei denen seine Person völlig aus dem Spiele blieb. Wie hätte ein Geist wie der seine dies Element nicht einschließen sollen! Daß er es tat, dafür waren Beweis genug seine Wiedergabe gewisser von Kretzschmar über-nommener Lehren über die Unverächtlichkeit des Sinnlichen in der Kunst, und nicht nur in dieser;

195   es zeugte von einem freien und gelassenen Ins-Auge-Fassen der Welt der Begierde.

200   die Intuition des Neulings den Sieg davontrug

203   einen Gezeichneten, vom Pfeil des Schicksals Getroffenen

204   der 'Bräunlichen' ... die sich ihm am Klavier genähert, und die er Esmeralda nannte ...

204	Einschlag von Liebesläuterung
205	etwas einer Liebesbindung Ähnliches
205-206	daß Liebe und Gift hier einmal für immer zur furchtbaren Erfahrungseinheit wurden: der mythologischen Einheit, welche der *Pfeil* verkörpert.

206   Die Unglückliche warnte den Verlangenden vor 'sich', das bedeutete einen Akt freier seelischer Erhebung über ihre erbarmungswürdige physische Existenz, einen Akt menschlicher Abstandsnahme davon, einen Akt der Rührung, — das Wort sei mir gewährt — einen Akt der Liebe. Und, gütiger Himmel, war es nicht Liebe auch, oder was war es, welche Versessenheit, welcher Wille zum gottversuchenden Wagnis, welcher Trieb, die Strafe in die Sünde einzubeziehen, endlich: welches tief geheimste Verlangen nach dämonischer Empfängnis, nach einer tödlich entfesselnden chymischen Veränderung seiner Natur wirkte dahin, daß der Gewarnte die Warnung verschmähte und auf dem Besitz dieses Fleisches bestand?

206   daß sie alle Süßigkeit ihres Weibtums aufbot, um ihn zu entschädigen für das, was er für sie wagte.

207   das schlagkräftige Opernwerk

207   ihr Name — derjenige, den er ihr von Anfang an gegeben — geistert runenhaft, von niemandem wahrgenommen als von mir, durch sein Werk. Möge man es mir als Eitelkeit auslegen, — ich kann es mir nicht versagen, schon hier der Entdeckung zu gedenken, die er mir eines Tages schweigend bestätigte.... . So findet sich in den Tongeweben meines Freundes eine fünf- bis sechsköpfige Notenfolge, mit h beginnend, mit es endigend und mit wechselndem e und a dazwischen, auffallend häufig wieder, eine motivische Grundfigur von eigentümlich schwermütigem Gepräge, die in vielfachen harmonischen und rhythmischen Einkleidungen, bald der, bald jener Stimme zugeteilt, oft in vertauschter Reihenfolge, gleichsam um ihre Achse gedreht, so daß bei gleichbleibenden Intervallen die Abfolge der Töne verändert ist, darin ihr Wesen treibt:

207   zuerst in dem wohl schönsten der noch in Leipzig komponierten dreizehn Brentano-Gesänge, dem herzzerwühlenden Lied "O lieb Mädel, wie schlecht bist du," das ganz davon beherrscht ist, dann namentlich in dem Spätwerk, worin Kühnheit und Verzweiflung sich auf eine so einzigartige Weise mischen, der ... "Weheklag Dr. Fausti", wo sich noch mehr die Neigung zeigt, die melodischen Intervalle auch harmonisch-simultan zu bringen.

der Tonalität, des tempierten Systems, der traditionellen Musik selber

243 Leverkühn wollte sie auch alle zusammen immer als ein Ganzes, also als ein Werk betrachtet und behandelt wissen, das aus einer bestimmten stilistischen Konzeption, einem Grundlaut, der kongenialen Berührung mit einem bestimmten, wundersam hoch und tief verträumten Dichtergeist hervorgegangen war

245 ganz selten in aller Literatur haben Wort und Klang einander gefunden und bestätigt wie hier... . Dieses sich tröstend und trauernd Einander-die-Hand-Bieten der Töne, dieses verwandelnd-verwandt ineinander Verwoben- und Verschlungensein aller Dinge, — das ist sie, und Adrian Leverkühn ist ihr jugendlicher Meister.

245 Alles ist freundlich wohlwollend verbunden,
bietet sich tröstend und trauernd die Hand,
sind durch die Nächte die Lichter gewunden,
alles ist ewig im Innern verwandt.

248 daß Kopfschmerz ihn drückte

248 Opferfest der Magdschaft

249 "daß wir dem Teufel die fleischliche Vermischung weggepascht haben, indem wir ein Sakrament, das Sakrament der christlichen Ehe draus machten."

250 "Und sollen sein ein Fleisch"

255 ich werde dir sagen, was ich unter strengem Satz verstehe. Ich meine damit die vollständige Integrierung aller musikalischen Dimensionen, ihre Indifferenz gegeneinander kraft vollkommener Organisation.

255 "Weißt du ... wo ich einem strengen Satz am nächsten war? ... Einmal im Brentano-Cyklus ... 'O lieb Mädel'. Das ist ganz aus einer Grundgestalt, einer vielfach variablen Intervallreihe, den fünf Tönen h-e-a-e-es abgeleitet, Horizontale und Vertikale sind davon bestimmt und beherrscht, soweit das eben bei einem Grundmotiv von so beschränkter Notenzahl möglich ist. Es ist wie ein Wort, ein Schlüsselwort, dessen Zeichen überall in dem Lied zu finden sind und es gänzlich determinieren möchten. Es ist aber ein zu kurzes Wort und in sich zu wenig beweglich.

255 Kopfschmerzen

255-256 Man müßte von hier aus weitergehen und aus den zwölf Stufen des temperierten Halbton-Alphabets größere Wörter bilden, Wörter von zwölf Buchstaben, bestimmte Kombinationen und Interrelationen der zwölf Halbtöne, Reihenbildungen, aus denen das Stück, der einzelne Satz oder ein ganzes mehrsätziges Werk strikt abgeleitet werden müßte. Jeder Ton der gesamten Komposition, melodisch und harmonisch, müßte sich über seine Beziehung zu dieser vorbestimmten Grundreihe auszuweisen haben. Keiner dürfte wiederkehren, ehe alle anderen erschienen sind. Keiner dürfte auftreten, der nicht der Gesamtkonstruktion seine motivische Funktion erfüllte. Es gäbe keine freie Note mehr. Das würde ich strengen Satz nennen.

	Zur Nacht den kühlen Trank, Vergiftetest du mein Leben ..."
305	Es hat sich an der Wunde Die Schlange fest gesaugt ...
308	Schmerzen, die die kleine Seejungfrau, wie von schneidenden Messern, in ihren schönen Menschenbeinen hatte, als sie sie statt des Schwanzes erworben
309	"unsre bleiche Venus"
310	"es kam nicht zur Metastasierung ins Metaphysische, Meta-venerische, Metainfektiose"
311	"Esmeralda's Freund und Zuhalt"
311	"die Metaspirochaetose, das ist der meningeale Prozeß ... als hätten gewisse von den Kleinen eine Passion fürs Obere, eine besondere Vorliebe für die Kopfregion, die Meningen, die dura mater, das Hirnzelt und die Pia.... .
313	"Das Hauptwee, den Ansatzpunkt für die Messerschmerzen der kleinen Seejungfrau, hast du doch auch von ihm.... . Im übrigen, ich habe ganz recht gesprochen, um Osmose, um Liquordiffusion, um den Proliferationsvorgang, handelt sichs bei dem ganzen Zauber. Ihr habt da den Lumbalsack mit der pulsierenden Liquorsäule darin, der reicht ins Zerebrale, zu den Hirnhäuten, in deren Gewebe die schleichende venerische Meningitis am leisen, verschwiegenen Werke ist. Aber ins Innere, ins Parenchym könnten unsere Kleinen gar nicht gelangen, so sehr es sie dorthin zieht und so sehnlich sie dorthin gezogen werden, — ohne Liquordiffusion, die Osmose.... ."
318	"Eine Wallfahrt auf Erbsen"
322-323	"Es sollte der Teufel wohl was von Musik verstehen.... . Der [Kierkegaard] wußte Bescheid und verstand sich auf mein besondres Verhältnis zu dieser schönen Kunst, — der allerchristlichsten Kunst, wie er findet, — mit negativem Vorzeichen natürlich, vom Christentum zwar eingesetzt und entwickelt, aber verneint und ausgeschlossen als dämonisches Bereich, —.... . Eine hochtheologische Angelegenheit, die Musik — wie die Sünde es ist.... ."
323	"Wahre Leidenschaft gibt es nur im Ambiguosen und als Ironie."
323	"schöpferische, Genie spendende Krankheit, Krankheit, die hoch zu Roß die Hindernisse nimmt, in kühnem Rausch von Fels zu Felsen sprengt.... ."
324	"die Schmerzen der kleinen Seejungfrau"

325	"von den Schmerzensanzahlungen, die zwischenein fürs hohe Leben zu leisten ..."
327	"Heulen und Zähneklappern"
329	"Eine Sündhaftigkeit, so heillos, daß sie ihren Mann von Grund aus am Heile verzweifeln läßt, ist der wahrhaft theologische Weg zum Heil."
330	"die Heilige Geschrift ... mit den figuris, characteribus und incantationibus der Musik"
331	So richteten wirs dir mit Fleiß, daß du uns in die Arme liefst, will sagen: meiner Kleinen, der Esmeralda, und daß du dirs holtest, die Illumination, das Aphrodisiacum des Hirns... .
332	"Was ich mir zugezogen, und weswegen du willst, ich sei dir versprochen, — was ist denn die Quelle davon, sag, als die Liebe, wenn auch die von dir mit Zulassung Gottes vergiftete? Das Bündnis, worin wir nach deiner Behauptung stehen, hat ja selbst mit Liebe zu tun, du Dummkopf."
332	"Do, re, mi! ... Liebe ist dir verboten, insofern sie wärmt. Dein Leben soll kalt sein — darum darfst du keinen Menschen lieben... . Eine Gesamterkältung deines Lebens und deines Verhältnisses zu den Menschen liegt in der Natur der Dinge, — vielmehr sie liegt bereits in deiner Natur, wir auferlegen dir beileibe nichts Neues, die Kleinen machen nichts Neues und Fremdes aus dir, sie verstärken und übertreiben nur sinnreich alles, was du bist. Ist etwa die Kälte bei dir nicht vorgebildet, so gut wie das väterliche Hauptwee, aus dem die Schmerzen der kleinen Seejungfrau werden sollen?"
332	"Kalt wollen wir dich, daß kaum die Flammen der Produktion heiß genug sein sollen, dich darin zu wärmen."
334	von Adrians Notenpapier in mein Manuskript zu übertragen
340	mistfüßige Stallmagd (Waltpurgis)
345	Das Geschlechtliche amüsierte ihn in einem literarischen Sinn; sexus und Geist hingen ihm eng zusammen ...
345	Er tat damals die Äußerung, daß die Beschäftigung mit diesen Liedern eine entschiedene und fast gefährliche *Verwöhnung* bedeute: Nicht leicht wolle einem etwas anderes von der Gattung danach noch gefallen.... das Außergewöhnliche und an allem anderen den Geschmack Verderbende ihn zuletzt in die Disintegration, ins Unmachbare, nicht mehr zu Bewerkstelligende treiben müsse.
349	" 'dezimierende Musik' "

350	Diesen geheimnisvoll anstößigen Versen nun hatte der Komponist sehr simple Harmonien verliehen, die im Verhältnis zu der Tonsprache des Ganzen — "falscher", zerrissener, unheimlicher wirkten als die gewagtesten Spannungen, tatsächlich das Ungeheuerlich-Werden des Dreiklangs erfahren ließen.
350	ein zukunftshaltiges Werk voll tiefer Musik
350	" 'ein gottgeistiger Mensch' "
369	Wagners Werk ... laut und heftig wie es war... .
395	als Dr. Helmut sich ihr, der Mann dem Weibe, genähert und um sie zu werben begonnen hatte. Ich war überzeugt und bin es geblieben, daß Ines sich nie in Schwerdtfeger verliebt hätte ohne den Eintritt Institoris', des Freiers, in ihr Leben. Der warb um sie, aber er tat es gewissermaßen für einen anderen.
396	Gegen Institoris, einen bloßen Dozenten des Schönen, hatte er den Vorteil der Kunst selbst, dieser Nährerin der Leidenschaft und Verklärerin des Menschlichen, auf seiner Seite. Denn die Person des Geliebten wird natürlich dadurch erhöht, und die Gefühle für ihn ziehen begreiflicherweise immer wieder neue Nahrung daraus, wenn mit dem Eindruck seiner Person fast stets berauschende Kunsteindrücke verbunden sind.
417	wie fast alle Juden, sehr musikalisch ...
424	"O Gregorius, du Mann Gottes... ."
425-426	Travestie, da er [der künstlerische Anreiz] dem kritischen Rückschlage entsprang auf die geschwollene Pathetik einer zu Ende gehenden Kunstepoche. Das musikalische Drama hatte seine Stoffe der romantischen Sage, der Mythenwelt des Mittelalters entnommen und dabei zu verstehen gegeben, daß nur dergleichen Gegenstände der Musik würdig, ihrem Wesen angemessen seien. Dem schien hier Folge geleistet: auf eine recht destruktive Weise jedoch, indem das Skurrile, besonders auch im Erotischen Possenhafte, an die Stelle moralischer Priesterlichkeit trat, aller inflationärer Pomp der Mittel abgeworfen und die Aktion der an sich schon burlesken Gliederpuppen-Bühne übertragen wurde.
425	" 'Der Teufel dachte uns zur Hölle zu führen, doch Gottes Übermacht hat es verhindert.' "
457	Es ist viel beruhigender, zu wissen, daß man nach dem Tode zu Schaum auf dem Meere wird, wie es der Kleinen von Natur wegen zukommt.
463	so schwere Kopfschmerzen
464	genau in der richtigen Tonart

465	"Ich habe sie niemals geliebt, ... ich hatte immer nur brüderlich-kameradschaftliche Empfindungen für sie ..."
465	nur Kavalierspflichten erfülle
466	Reinigung
466-467	"Wunderbar würden Sie es machen, ... mit einem unerhört einfachen und sangbaren ersten Thema im Hauptsatz, das nach der Kadenz wieder einsetzt, — ... Aber Sie brauchen es gar nicht so zu machen, Sie brauchen überhaupt keine Kadenz zu machen, das ist ja ein Zopf. Sie können alle Konventionen umstoßen und auch die Satzeinteilung, — es braucht gar keine Sätze zu haben, meinetwegen könnte das Allegro molto in der Mitte stehen, ein wahrer Teufelstriller, bei dem du mit dem Rhythmus jonglierst, wie nur Sie es können, und das Adagio könnte zum Schluß kommen, als Verklärung — es wäre zwischen uns wie ein Kind, ein platonisches Kind, — ja, unser Konzert, das wäre so recht die Erfüllung von allem, was ich unter platonisch verstehe."
467	sein tragisches Ende
467	auf die Dauer erwies sich die Wehrlosigkeit der Einsamkeit gegen solche Werbung, allerdings zu des Werbers Verderben.
467	ein platonisches Kind
472	Genie ist eine in der Krankheit tief erfahrene, aus ihr schöpfende und durch sie schöpferische Form der Lebenskraft.
475	die große Erzhure, das Weib auf dem Tiere ...
475	Portraitstudie einer venezianischen Kurtisane ...
476	körperstrotzend ... Charons Nachen sich seiner Last entlädt ... der Verdammte, üppig in Fleisch ... gräßliche Abfahrt hält
476	Engel hier in die Posaunen des Untergangs stoßen... .
476	die Gnade zwei Sünderseelen noch aus dem Falle ins Heil emporzieht
496	Sprechchöre ... zur reichsten Vokal-Musik werden ... begleitet von Klängen, die als bloßes Geräusch, als magisch-fanatisch-negerhaftes Trommeln und Gong-Dröhnen beginnen und bis zu höchster Musik reichen ...
496	das Verborgenste musikalisch zu enthüllen, das Tier im Menschen wie seine sublimsten Regungen
498	Die Stimme der babylonischen Hure, des Weibes auf dem Tiere, mit welcher gebuhlt zu haben die Könige auf Erden, ist seltsam überraschender Weise dem graziösesten Koloratursopran übertragen, und ihre virtuosen Läufe gehen zuweilen mit vollkommen flötenhafter Wirkung in den Orchesterklang ein.
498	der Chor ist instrumentalisiert, das Orchester vokalisiert

502	mir das tiefste Geheimnis der Musik, welches ein Geheimnis der Identität ist, auf eine das Herz stockenlassende Weise offenbart hätte
502	in der Verungleichung des Gleichen ...
502-503	Das zuvor vernommene Schrecknis ist zwar in dem unbeschreiblichen Kinderchor in eine gänzlich andere Lage übertragen zwar völlig uminstrumentiert und umrhythmisiert; aber in dem sirrenden, sehrenden Spähren- und Engelsgetön ist *keine* Note, die nicht, streng korrespondierend, auch in dem Höllengelächter vorkäme.
517	jener zarten ... Liebe
517	der Sphäre der Liebe und des Glaubens, des Ewig-Weiblichen mit einem Wort... .
517	die intellektuelle Höhe und religiösen Gehalte, den Stolz und die Verzweiflung, die sündige, ins Inspirative getriebene Klugheit der Musik ...
519	durch den asketischen Verzicht auf jede direkte Annäherung
520	ruft es die Vorstellung der Wall- und Pilgerfahrt wach ...
521	einer Schutzgöttin, einer Egeria, einer geisterhaften Geliebten?
521	Unheilige, fliehet! Entweichet!
521	dessen hervorschießende Zunge die ausgebildete Gestalt eines Pfeiles hatte
542	ein wenig aus dem Rahmen von Leverkühns unerbittlich radikalem und zugeständnislosem Gesamtwerk
543	an der Grenze des Spottes gehaltenen Süße und Zärtlichkeit
543	Es ist ein in seiner Art wundervoller melodischer Wurf, eine rauschende, in großem Bogen sich hintragende, sinnbenehmende Kantilene, die entschieden etwas Etalagehaftes, Prunkhaftes hat, dazu eine Melancholie, der es an Gefälligkeit, nach dem Sinne des Spielers, nicht fehlt.
543-544	Das Charakteristisch-Entzückende der Erfindung ist das unerwartete und zart akzentuierte Sichübersteigern der auf einen gewissen Höhepunkt gelangten melodischen Linie um eine weitere Tonstufe, von der sie dann, mit höchstem Geschmack, vielleicht allzuviel Geschmack geführt, zurückflutend sich aussingt. Es ist eine der schon körperlich wirkenden, Haupt und Schultern hinnehmenden, das "Himmlische" streifenden Schönheitsmanifestationen, deren nur die Musik und sonst keine Kunst fähig ist. Und die Tutti-Verherrlichung eben dieses Themas im letzten Teil des Variationensatzes bringt den Ausbruch ins offene C-Dur. Dem Eclat voran geht eine Art von

kühnem Anlauf in dramatischem Parlando-Charakter, — eine deutliche Reminiszenz an das Rezitativ der Primgeige im letzten Satz von Beethovens a-Moll-Quartett, — nur daß auf die großartige Phrase dort etwas anderes folgt als eine melodische Festivität, in der die Parodie des Hinreißenden ganz ernst gemeinte und darum irgendwie beschämend wirkende Leidenschaft wird.

140

Quotations

579	"In meinem Leben war einer, dessen beherztes Ausharren — man kann beinahe sagen: den Tod überwand; der das Menschliche in mir frei machte, mich das Glück lehrte."
581	"Das ist eine Idee von mir, ein Einfall, wie er einem beim Komponieren kommt."
582	"Er hat nun einmal in meinen Augen mit Liebesdingen nichts zu tun."
583	"Schon in Zürich — ich hatte gespielt — ich hatte *dich* gespielt und war warm und empfänglich — hat sie's mir angetan."
583-584	"Ich habe dich zu diesem Liebesdienst ersehen, weil du dabei weit mehr in deinem Element bist als, sagen wir, Serenus Zeitblom."
584	"Du wirst aus eigener Empfindung sprechen — für mich und meine Absicht. Unmöglich kann ich mir einen berufeneren, erwünschteren Werber denken."
586	Er hatte Freund und Geliebte auf einmal verloren....
586	die unleugbare erotische Anziehungskraft
587	für einen Fanatiker des Flirts
588	Wie bekennt man einer Frau die Liebe eines andern?
589	das Violinkonzert sei ihm gewidmet, aber letzten Endes sei es das Mittel gewesen, den Komponisten ihrer ansichtig werden zu lassen.
591	Aber es ist müßig, sich über die Zukunft, die Glücksaussichten einer Verbindung Gedanken zu machen, der keine Zukunft bestimmt war, sondern die von einem gewalttätigen Schicksal rasch zunichte gemacht werden sollte.
592	unmusikalisch
601	Besonders gern sah er damals die elegante Bäuerin bei sich: sie besaß für ihn nun einmal eine wohltätig beruhigende Gegenwart, eine Art von beschützender Kraft, und tatsächlich habe ich ihn mit ihr in einem Winkel der Abtsstube *Hand in Hand* sitzen sehen, schweigend und wie geborgen. Dies Hand in Hand sah ihm nicht gleich, es war eine Veränderung, die ich mit Rührung, sogar mit Freude, aber auch nicht ganz ohne Ängstlichkeit wahrnahm.
603	Schwere Migräneanfälle hielten ihn im Dunkel ...
605	" 'keine Sonate schreiben wollen, sondern einen Roman' "
611	Besuch aus niedlicher Klein- und Feinwelt
611	Elfenprinzchen
611	sein selbstverständlich von Koketterie und Wissen um seinen Zauber nicht ganz freies Lächeln

612	die Untauglichkeit der Sprache ... Sichtbarkeit zu erreichen, ein wirklich genaues Bild des Individuellen hervorzubringen
615	"Gotteskindlein" ... vom Himmel gefallen sei.
616	auf diese Manier müßten die Englein droben die Seiten ihrer Hallelujabücher wenden.
618	Ein Schwertfisch, ein Sägefisch und Hai —
618	solcher Behandlung mit der Ironie zu begegnen, mit der Nepo meinen pädagogischen Anlauf beobachtet hatte.
618-619	jener Elfenspott schien der Ausdruck des Wissens davon
620	Hand in Hand
623	drei wohlharmonisierte kleine Biedermeier-Melodien, denen Echo in immer gleichem Gebanntsein lauschte, mit Augen, in denen Amüsiertheit, Erstaunen und tief schauende Träumerei sich auf unvergeßliche Weise mischten.
623	Auch des Onkels Handschriften, diese über die Liniensysteme hingestreuten, mit Fähnchen und Federchen geschmückten, durch Bögen und Balken verbundenen, leeren und schwarzen Runen... .
623	betrachtete er gern und ließ sich erklären, wovon etwa mit all den Zeichen die Rede war: — von ihm, unter uns gesagt... . Dies Kind, vor uns allen zuerst, durfte "Einblick" nehmen in die Partiturskizze von Ariels Liedern aus dem "Tempest", an denen Leverkühn damals heimlich arbeitete ...
624	die schwebende, kindlich-hold-verwirrende Leichtigkeit Ariels
624	der gute Zaubermeister
624	weil die Migräne ihn in die Stille, ja ins Dunkle zwang
629-630	die unsinnigen Kopfschmerzen
630	schädelsprengende Schmerzen
630	der typische "hydrocephale Schrei"
630	schreiender, sich bäumender Folter
630	Himmelsaugen
630	herzzerreißendes Lamentieren
630	mit dem Zähneknirschen
632-632	"Nimm seinen Leib, über den du Gewalt hast! Wirst mir seine süße Seele doch hübsch zufrieden lassen müssen, und das ist deine Ohnmacht und dein Ridikül, mit dem ich dich ausspotten will Äonen lang. Mögen auch Ewigkeiten gewälzt sein zwischen meinen Ort und seinen, ich werde doch wissen, daß er ist, von wo du hinausgeworfen wurdest, Dreckskerl... .
639	die letzten Jahre des geistigen Leben meines Helden, diese beiden Jahre 1929 und 30, nach dem Scheitern seines Ehe-

Planes, dem Verlust des Freundes, der Hinwegnahme des wunderbaren Kindes... .

641 diese ... qualvollen Migräneattacken

642 die eine Tristan-Stelle wörtlich vorwegnimmt

643 die Wiedergewinnung, ich möchte nicht sagen und sage es um der Genauigkeit willen doch: die Rekonstruktion des Ausdrucks, der höchsten und tiefsten Ansprechung des Gefühls auf einer Stufe der Geistigkeit und der Formenstrenge, die erreicht werden mußte, damit dieses Umschlagen kalkulatorischer Kälte in den expressiven Seelenlaut und kreatürlich sich anvertrauende Herzlichkeit Ereignis werden könne... .

644 die Nymphen-Klage

644 Nicht umsonst knüpft die Faustus-Kantate stilistisch so stark und unverkennbar an Monteverdi und das siebzehnte Jahr-hundert an, dessen Musik — wiederum nicht umsonst — die Echo-Wirkung, zuweilen bis zur Manier, bevorzugte: ... In Leverkühns letzter und höchster Schöpfung aber ist dieses Lieblingsdessin des Barock, das Echo, oftmals mit unsäglich schwermütiger Wirkung verwendet.

644-645 Ich will hier den Leser zurückverweisen auf das Gespräch, das ich eines schon fernen Tages, am Hochzeitstage seiner Schwester zu Buchel, auf einem Spaziergang die Kuhmulde entlang, mit Adrian hatte, und wobei er mir, unter dem Druck von Kopfschmerzen, seine Idee eines "strengen Satzes" entwickelte, abgeleitet aus der Art, wie in dem Liede "O lieb Mädel, wie schlecht bist du" Melodie und Harmonie von der Abwandlung eines fünftönigen Grundmotivs, des Buchstaben-symbols h e a e es, bestimmt sind.

645 die substantielle Identität des Seligsten mit dem Gräßlichsten, die innere Einerleiheit des Engelskinder-Chors mit dem Höllengelächter

646 Es liegt zum Grunde allem, was da klingt, — besser: es liegt, als Tonart fast, hinter allem und schafft die Identität des Vielförmigsten, — jene Identität, die zwischen dem kristallenen Engelschor und dem Höllengejohle der "Apokalypse" waltet, und die nun allumfassend geworden ist: zu einer Formveranstaltung von letzter Rigorosität, die nichts Unthematisches mehr kennt, in der die Ordnung des Materials total wird ... eben weil es keine freie Note mehr gibt.

647 im Sinne des Résumés

648	Längst vorhergesagt ist in diesen Blättern, daß im "Faustus" auch jenes Buchstabensymbol, die von mir zuerst wahrgenommene Hetæra-esmeralda-Figur, das h e a e es, sehr oft Melodik und Harmonik beherrscht: überall da nämlich, wo von der Verschreibung und Versprechung, dem Blut-Rezeß, nur immer die Rede ist.
648	deren Kern, aus dem alles entwickelt ist, eben das zwölftönige ... bildet
650	mit der sprechenden Unausgesprochenheit, welche nur der Musik gegeben ist ...
651	wie, wenn der künstlerischen Paradoxie ... das religiöse Paradoxon entspräche, daß aus tiefster Heillosigkeit, wenn auch als leiseste Frage nur, die Hoffnung keimte?
651	als ein Licht in der Nacht
651	das hohe g eines Cellos, das letzte Wort, der letzte verschwebende Laut, in Pianissimo-Fermate langsam vergehend
651	Dann ist nichts mehr, — Schweigen und Nacht. Aber der nachschwingend im Schweigen hängende Ton, der nicht mehr ist, dem nur die Seele noch nachlauscht, und der Ausklang der Trauer war, ist es nicht mehr, wandelt den Sinn, steht als ein Licht in der Nacht.
660	"Denn es war nur ein Schmetterling und eine bunte Butterfliege, Hetæra Esmeralda, die hatt es mir angetan durch Berührung, die Milchhexe, und folgt ihr nach in den dämmernden Laubschatten, den ihre durchsichtige Nacktheit liebt, und wo ich sie haschte, die im Flug einem windgeführten Blütenblatt gleicht, haschte sie und koste mit ihr, ihrer Warnung zum Trotz, so war es geschehen. Denn wie sie mir's angetan, so tat sie mir's an und vergab mir in der Liebe —"
661	"Denn lange schon bevor ich mit dem giftigen Falter koste, war meine Seel in Hochmut und Stolz zu dem Satan unterwegs gewesen...."
664	"Hatte wohl auch gedacht, schon zuvor, daß ich, als des Teufels Mönch, lieben dürfte in Fleisch und Blut, was nicht weiblich war, der aber um mein Du in grenzenloser Zutraulichkeit warb, bis ich's ihm gewährte. Darum mußt ich ihn töten und schickte ihn in den Tod nach Zwang und Weisung.
667	in stark dissonantem Akkorde
676	eine unkenntlich verschleierte Fremde, die, während die Erdschollen auf den eingebetteten Sarg fielen, wieder verschwunden war.

Select Bibliography

I.   Bibliographical Listings of Secondary Literature on *Doctor Faustus*:

Jonas, Klaus W. *Fifty Years of Thomas Mann Studies: A Bibliography of Criticism*. Minneapolis: University of Minnesota Press, 1955. 174-86.

Jonas, Klaus W. and Ilsedore B. Jonas. *Thomas Mann Studies*. Volume II: *A Bibliography of Criticism*. Philadelphia: University of Pennsylvania Press, 1967. 394 (references to studies of *Doctor Faustus* listed throughout the volume).

Jonas, Klaus W. *Die Thomas-Mann Literatur*. Band I: *Bibliographie der Kritik 1896-1955*. Berlin: Erich Schmidt, 1972. 421-22 (references to studies of *Doctor Faustus* listed throughout the volume).

Jonas, Klaus W. *Die Thomas-Mann Literatur*. Band II: *Bibliographie der Kritik 1956-1975*. Berlin: Erich Schmidt, 1979. 649-50 (references to studies of *Doctor Faustus* listed throughout volumes I and II).

Matter, Harry. *Die Literatur über Thomas Mann. Eine Bibliographie 1898-1969*. Vol. I. Berlin & Weimar: Aufbau, 1972. 511-70.

Wolff, Rudolf. "Bibliographie von 1947 bis 1968 (Auswahl)" In *Thomas Manns 'Doktor Faustus,' und die Wirkung*. 1. Teil. Ed. Rudolf Wolff. Sammlung Profile, vol. 4. Bonn: Bouvier, 1983. 152-67.

Wolff, Rudolf. "Bibliographie von 1968 bis 1983 (Auswahl)" In *Thomas Manns 'Doktor Faustus,' und die Wirkung*. Teil II. Ed. Rudolf Wolff. Sammlung Profile, vol. 5. Bonn: Bouvier, 1983. 152-67.

In view of the comprehensive and relatively complete bibliographical background on Thomas Mann's *Doctor Faustus* available in the sources listed above and in individual monographs on the novel cited in the text, the following select bibliography will only list those studies of the work which treat one or more of the central elements — music, love or death — forming the focal point of this investigation. Neither unpublished doctoral dissertations nor newspaper articles are included.

II.   Studies of Melos, Eros, Thanatos and *Doctor Faustus*

Albrecht, Ján. "Leverkühn oder die Musik als Schicksal." *Deutsche Vierteljahrsschrift für Literaturwissenschaft und Geistesgeschichte* 45 (1971): 375-88.

Aronson, Alex. "The Musical Erotic" and "The Devil's Disciple." In *Music and the Novel: A Study in Twentieth-Century Fiction.* Totowa, New Jersey: Rowman and Littlefield, 1980. 110-36 and 182-215.

Bergsten, Gunilla. "Musical Symbolism in Thomas Mann's *Doctor Faustus.*" *Orbis litterarum* 14 (1959): 206-14.

Boyer, Jean. "A propos du rôle de la musique dans le *Doctor Faustus* de Thomas Mann." *Annales de la Faculté des Lettres de Toulouse.* December, 1951. 118-43.

Brode, Hanspeter. "Musik und Zeitgeschichte im Roman: Thomas Manns *Doktor Faustus.*" *Jahrbuch der Deutschen Schillergesellschaft* 17 (1974): 455-72.

Buzga, Jaroslav. "Leverkühn und die moderne Musik." *Melos* 32, Nr. 2: 37-41.

Carnegy, Patrick. *Faust as Musician. A Study of Thomas Mann's Novel 'Doctor Faustus.'* London: Chatto and Windus, 1973.

Cerf, Steven. "Love in Thomas Mann's *Doctor Faustus* as an Imitatio Shakespeari." *Comparative Literature Studies* 18 (1981): 475-86.

Cotterill, Rowland. "Hesitant Allegory: Music in Thomas Mann's *Doctor Faustus.*" *Comparison* 7 (1977): 58-91.

Dahlhaus, Carl. "Fiktive Zwölftonmusik. Thomas Mann und Theodor W. Adorno." *Jahrbuch der Deutschen Akademie für Sprache und Dichtung* 1 (1982): 33-49.

Dück, Hans-Udo. "Epische Symphonik in Thomas Manns *Doktor Faustus.*" In *Vergleichen und verändern. Festschrift für Helmut Motekat.* Ed. Albrecht Goetze and Günther Pflaum, Munich: Hueber. 1970. 243-58.

Engel, Hans. "Musik der Krise, Krise der Musik, oder *Doktor Faustus*. Zu Thomas Manns Roman." *Neue Musik-Zeitschrift* 3 (1949): 336-42.

Engelberg, Edward. "Thomas Manns Faust und Beethoven." *Monatshefte* 47 (1955): 112-16.

Engelmann, Hans Ulrich. "Joseph Berglinger und Adrian Leverkühn oder: über die Wärme und über die Kälte." *Neue Zeitschrift für Musik* 124 (1963): 470-73.

Ezergailis, Inta Miske. *Male and Female: An Approach to Thomas Mann's Dialectic*. The Hague: Nijhoff, 1975.

Fetzer, John F. "Nachklänge Brentanoscher Musik in Thomas Manns *Doktor Faustus*." In *Clemens Brentano. Beiträge des Kolloquiums im Freien Deutschen Hochstift 1978*, ed. Detlev Lüders. Tübingen: Niemeyer, 1980. 33-46.

Feuerlicht, Ignace. "Thomas Mann and Homoeroticism." *Germanic Review* 57 (1982): 89-97.

Field, G(eorge) W. "Music and Morality in Thomas Mann and Hermann Hesse." *University of Toronto Quarterly* 24 (1955): 175-90.

Fischer, Erika. "Adrian Leverkühns Philosophie der Neuen Musik." *Literatur für Leser: Zeitschrift für Interpretationspraxis und geschichtliche Texterkenntnis* (1984): 162-70.

Förster, Wolf-Dietrich. "Leverkühn, Schönberg und Thomas Mann. Musikalische Strukturen und Kunstreflexion in *Doktor Faustus*." *Deutsche Vierteljahresschrift für Literaturwissenschaft und Geistesgeschichte* 49 (1975): 694-720.

Gandelman, Claude. "La 'musique de sable' des Leverkühns; une métaphore nietzschéenne cachée dans le *Doktor Faustus* de Thomas Mann." *Deutsche Vierteljahrsschrift für Literaturwissenschaft und Geistesgeschichte* 52 (1978): 511-20.

Hamburger, Paul. "Thomas Mann's *Dr. Faustus*: A Contribution to the Philosophy of Music." *Music Survey* 2 (1949): 20-24.

Hansen, Mathias. "Thomas Mann und Arnold Schönberg — schöpferische Beziehungen zwischen Dichtung und Musik." *Akademie der Künste der*

Deutschen Demokratischen Republik. Sektion Musik. Arbeitsheft Nr. 24 (1976): 88-103.

Hatfield, Henry. "Death in the Late Works of Thomas Mann." *Germanic Review* 34 (1959): 284-88.

Heimann, Bodo. "Thomas Manns *Doktor Faustus* und die Musikphilosophie Adornos." *Deutsche Vierteljahrsschrift für Literaturwissenschaft und Geistesgeschichte* 38 (1964): 248-66.

Herz, Gerhard. "The Music in Mann's *Doctor Faustus.*" *Perspectives* 3 (1948): 48-64.

Hirschbach, Frank. "Devil's Jig on Hallowed Ground." In *The Arrow and the Lyre: A Study of the Role of Love in the Works of Thomas Mann.* The Hague: Nijhoff, 1955. 115-48.

Hofe, Gerhard vom. "Das unbehagliche Bewußtsein des modernen Musikers. Zu Wackenroders Berglinger und Thomas Manns *Doktor Faustus.*" In *Geist und Zeichen. Festschrift für Arthur Henkel.* Ed. Herbert Anton, Bernhard Gajek and Peter Pfaff. Heidelberg: Winter, 1977. 144-56.

Jung, Jürgen. *Altes und Neues zu Thomas Manns Roman 'Doktor Faustus'. Quellen und Modelle. Mythos, Psychologie, Musik, Theo-Dämonologie, Faschismus.* Europäische Hochschulschriften, Reihe 1, vol. 821. Frankfurt am Main: Lang, 1985.

Keiichi, Aisawa. *Ironie und Musik in Thomas Manns 'Doktor Faustus'.* Tokyo: Deutsches Seminar der Universität, 1983.

Kneipel, Eberhard. "Thomas Manns Version der Schönbergschen Zwölftontechnik im *Doktor Faustus.*" In *Thomas Mann. Werk und Wirkung.* Ed. Helmut Brandt and Hans Kaufmann. Berlin: Aufbau, 1978. 273-83.

Kohlschmidt, Werner. "Musikalität, Reformation und Deutschtum in Thomas Manns *Doktor Faustus.* In *Die entzweite Welt. Studien zum Menschenbild in der neueren Dichtung.* Gladbeck: Freizeiten-Verlag, 1953. 98-112.

Kolago, Lech. "Nachklänge der Musikgeschichte im Roman *Doktor Faustus* von Thomas Mann." *Germanica-Wratislaviensia* 36 (1980): 193-201.

Select Bibliography

Krey, Johannes. "Die gesellschaftliche Bedeutung der Musik im Werk von Thomas Mann." *Wissenschaftliche Zeitschrift der Friedrich Schiller-Universität Jena. Gesellschafts- und sprachwissenschaftliche Reihe* 3 (1953): 317-31.

Lyon, James K. "Words and Music. Thomas Mann's Tone-Poem *Doctor Faustus.*" *Western Humanities Review* 13 (1959): 99-102.

Mann, Michael. "The Musical Symbolism in Thomas Mann's *Doctor Faustus.*" *Music Review* 17 (1956): 314-22.

Myers, David. "Sexual Love and Caritas in Thomas Mann." *Journal of English and Germanic Philology* 68 (1969): 593-604.

Müller-Blattau, Joseph M. "Die Musik in Thomas Manns *Doktor Faustus* und Hermann Hesses *Glasperlenspiel.*" *Annales Universitatis Saraviensis* 2 (1953): 145-54.

Omori, Goro. "Liebe und Tod bei Thomas Mann." *Doitsu Bungaku — Die deutsche Literatur.* Nr. 4 (1967): 57-93; Nr. 5 (1967): 37-63 (in Japanese with German summary).

Oswald, Victor A. "Thomas Mann and the Mermaid. A Note in Constructivistic Music." *Modern Language Notes* 65 (1950): 171-75.

Pringsheim, Klaus. "Der Tonsetzer Adrian Leverkühn. Ein Musiker über Thomas Manns Roman." *Der Monat* 1 (1949): 84-91.

Pringsheim, Klaus. "The Music of Adrian Leverkühn." *Musicology* 2 (1949): 255-68.

Puschmann, Rosemarie. *Magisches Quadrat und Melancholie in Thomas Manns 'Doktor Faustus.' Von der musikalischen Struktur zum semantischen Beziehungsnetz.* Bielefeld: AMPAL Verlag, 1983.

Reinhardt, George W. "Thomas Mann's *Doctor Faustus*: A Wagnerian Novel." *Mosaic* 18 (1985): 109-23.

Rose, Marilyn Gaddis. "More on the Musical Composition of *Doctor Faustus.*" *Modern Fiction Studies* 17 (1971): 81-89.

Schädlich, Michael. *Thomas Mann und das christliche Denken. Eine Untersuchung über den Zusammenhang von Theologie und Musik im 'Doktor Faustus.'* Berlin: A. Kietz, 1963.

Scher, Steven Paul. "Thomas Mann's Verbal Score: Adrian Leverkühn's Symbolic Confession. " *Modern Language Notes* 82 (1967): 403-20. See also Scher, *Verbal Music in German Literature.* New Haven: Yale University Press, 1968. 106-42.

Schlee, Agnes. *Wandlungen musikalischer Strukturen im Werke Thomas Manns. Vom Leitmotiv zur Zwölftonreihe.* Europäische Hochschulschriften, Reihe 1, vol. 384. Frankfurt am Main: Lang, 1981.

Sommerhage, Claus. *Eros und Poesis. Über das Erotische im Werk Thomas Manns.* Bonn: Bouvier, 1983, 238-77: "Anstelle eines Ausblicks. Abschließender Exkurs über den *Doktor Faustus.*"

Starzycki, Andrzej. "Thomas Mann's *Doctor Faustus.* A Contribution to the Studies of Musical Facts in Literature." *Zagadnienia Rodzajów Literackich* 7 (1964): 27-41.

Stein, Jack M. "Adrian Leverkühn as a Composer," *Germanic Review* 25 (1950): 257-74.

Timm, Eitel. "Thomas Manns Doktor Faustus im Film: Zum Problem der 'Wortmusik.' " *Carleton Germanic Papers* 15 (1987): 41-54.

Wehrmann, Harald. *Thomas Manns 'Doktor Faustus'. Von den fiktiven Werken Adrian Leverkühns zur musikalischen Struktur des Romans.* Frankfurt am Main: Lang, 1988.

Wörner, Karl H. "Ein Dichter über Musik. Thomas Mann in seinem Roman *Doktor Faustus.*" *Musica* 2 (1948): 229-37.

Wootton, Carol. "Ferruccino Busoni's Opera *Doktor Faust*, Seen in Relation to Literary Interpretations of the Theme." In Wootton, *Selective Affinities. Comparative Essays from Goethe to Arden.* New York: Lang, 1983. 99-112.

Zuckerkandl, Victor. "Die Musik des *Doktor Faustus.*" *Neue Rundschau* 49 (1948): 203-14.

Index